BASTARD IN

by Jeff Jacklin

Text copyright © 2014 Jeff Jacklin

All Rights Reserved

Dedication

This book is dedicated to referees everywhere in the certain knowledge that you will not be Man of the Match in your game this weekend.

BASTARD IN BLACK

Preface

This book is a mixture of original and true tales from the long experience of the author in trudging the football pitches in the parks around England stretching to exaggerated anecdotes about reffing at all levels interspersed with funnies and semi-serious refereeing matters.

Don't be misled by the title, that's designed to get you past the cover (and it worked), as this book is very much on the side of the much maligned park referee and presents a hugely biased case that this endangered species deserves every football fans endearing gratitude.

This book is not just aimed at referees, if you are interested in any aspect of football then you will be able to relate to the individuals you meet throughout this book.

Park referees obviously cannot take themselves too seriously or they would all be on very strong medication and this book attempts to portray the thinking that makes a grown man dress up in black shirt and shorts, face a force nine gale, a whinging touch-line of ignorant supporters and relatives and then try and bring some semblance of control over 22 younger men running around trying to kick seven bells out of each other. It's a grand way to spend a Sunday morning.

Table of Contents

1 - Pre Match Briefing

2 - First Impressions, Second Thoughts

3 - The Day I Ref'd in Broadmoor and Escaped to Tell the Tale

4 - I Knew It Was Going To Be A Bad Game When

5 - How To Drop The Referee In The Fertiliser

6 - The Craic In The Changing Room

7 - A Game of Two Halves

8 - Diary of a Referee's Season

9 - The Old Farts League Rules

10 - In Defence of the Referee

11 - Becoming an X-Rated Referee

12 - The Cardboard Cut-Out Ref

13 - Everybody has a Ref Story to Tell

14 - Man Management Skills or a Cop Out?

15 - Shove A Whistle in It!

16 - The Early Laws of Association Football

17 - Life Without Referees

18 - Things You No Longer See At Football Grounds

19 - Refereeing Acronyms

20 - The Flexible Rules of Playground Football

21 - Ten Things We Really Love To See At A Football Match

22 - World Cup 2014: The Alternative Team Squads

23 - Refereeing Horoscopes

24 - Twenty Reasons Why Sex Is Better Than Football

25 - American Football is Dead

26 - The Startrek Page

27 - Referee Quiz Time

28 - Old News

29 - Extra Time

30 - Problem Page

Quiz Answers

1 - Pre Match Briefing

What this book is all about

This book is dedicated to the local parks referee in an attempt to show to football fans that we do indeed have feelings and a sense of humour. After being involved in parks football for over 40 years, 20 years playing, 5 years managing teams and 15 years refereeing, I feel eminently qualified to present the case for the defence of the average park referee or, as the terraces chant would have you believe, the Bastard in Black.

I've related this to the equivalent of the football fan's fanzine but retitled it a Refzine. You may well be familiar with, and even read, fanzines. These are cheaply produced magazines about a particular club written by supporters. They have largely been overtaken by new technology nowadays with the Unofficial Club Websites springing up to replace the printed version but some still remain. These fanzines regularly lambast their own team, manager, directors, chairman as well as the antics of neighbouring teams. They go to extremes - deeply critical one minute, highly supportive the next. This publication supports that contrasting approach to its subject.

A fanzine truly reflects the emotion of following your team through thick and thin. And throughout these publications, despite all the criticism and sarcastic wit, these same people will defend their team against any outside sniping whilst spending all their spare time and money travelling around the country in support of their loved ones.

One of the regular targets for fanzines is the much maligned referee and so it was decided that we in turn must group together to repel the masses who queue to ridicule our best mental and physical efforts. For too long the wave of criticism has been drowning out the wonderful job that most referees do week in week out for very little financial return. The tide must be turned, the balance must be redressed, Bastard in Black aims to do just that.

It's a Refzine about the feelings, tribulations, loneliness, intimidation, indecisiveness, lack of self-confidence that all referees feel at times. It's about conveying that to the supporters and players of teams whether they be in the plush stadiums or the local public park. It's all about offering the referee's point of view. And as in all good fanzines, there will be criticism, sarcasm, humour as well as support for the referee.

Many of the stories have come from articles I wrote when editing the Huddersfield Referee's Association monthly magazine in the mid/late nineties with an assortment of intermittent later tales and experiences.

They offer an insight to the real feelings of the man in black that most will never consider or be prepared to experience. For have no doubts about it, those who take up the whistle are the real football fanatics of this world. Not the fan who travels around the country in air conditioned coaches to a scheduled fixture list, sitting under cover with his match-day programme, cup of Bovril and meat pie after swilling back half a gallon of the local brew as part of his pre-match preparations.

The referee has probably spent many dark, wet winter evenings plodding the local streets to improve the stamina and fitness levels demanded of them every weekend. He's probably travelled alone to the game, had little recognition on arrival, will be treated with scant regard on the pitch, have to chase up his match fee, not be invited to the post match gathering and then set off alone on the return journey. And that's if he's had a good game! It gets worse, much worse.

Bastard in Black is about educating the masses about what it means to be the guy who will determine how the match will be played today - full scale war, easy-going, over-reactive or in good spirit. One thing is for sure the Bastard in Black will upset someone every time they step on to the pitch. Read on and find out what it really is like to be hated by following the highs and lows, experiences and tribulations of the Bastard in Black.

------- oooOooo ------

2 - First Impressions, Second Thoughts

The editor bravely recalls his first ever game in the middle

My first ever match as a referee was a total disaster. Newly qualified, bedecked in brand new kit ordered from the local sports shop and with a virgin whistle, I approached my first official appointment in total terror.

I was just seventeen and had qualified six weeks earlier with a creditable (I thought) 92.5% pass mark. Theory was one thing, practice, as I was soon to find out, was something totally different. My 92.5% stood for nothing as I took charge of Scawby Youth Club v Scunthorpe Youth Centre, Under-17 league match on a warm Sunday afternoon on the first October weekend.

My delayed start to the season was due to having to await the delivery of my new kit, which I hadn't the confidence to order in advance of the exam. This was in spite of my ex-League referee tutor, Cyril Leake, repeatedly proclaiming that he hadn't had a failure in 18 years of getting referees ready for such exams. The weekly lessons in his front room served the class of '65 (both of us) very well and the Scunthorpe Referees Association had two new recruits.

I contacted the fixture secretary upon delivery of the kit and advised him that the next Arthur Rowe was ready to honour the Scunthorpe Intermediate League by allowing them to place me with my maiden fixture. In due course a postcard arrived from Fixture Secretary, Ken Stones, giving me four fixtures over the coming month.

Scawby is a village six miles east of Scunthorpe, my home town. My cycle was out of commission and with no family car in those days, I warily resorted to the erratic ways of the Lincolnshire Road Car Bus Company to get me to this footballing outpost. Bus time-tabling is notably erratic in rural Lincolnshire, especially on Sundays, and I arrive eighty minutes before kick-off. Pleasant enough wait in the village park having subjected the pitch to a thorough examination and worked through Cyril's prescribed pre-match routine in preparation. I haven't tested the whistle out yet, hope it works, still I've got a spare, as per the text book - haven't tested that one either!

Thirty minutes to go and apart from an increasing number of mother escorted visitors to the children's swings there's no activity at all. I am here on the right day aren't I? Yes of course, so where is everyone? I wander across to the slide and make a casual enquiry of the friendliest looking of the mums on duty. 'Oh they don't play Sunday games here son, you need to be in Meadow Park on the other side of the village.'

Hastily obtaining directions I head off on foot, past emptying pubs as dads observe the ritual of being home for 2, because that's when the joint needs carving. Increasing speed past the war memorial and seated pensioners, who turn and look in curiosity, no-one runs through Scawby especially on a Sunday afternoon! I'm there, twenty minutes to kick-off. Not too bad I suppose and ample time to change, little further time to worry about the match itself, maybe that's a good thing.

Time to test this whistle out. In the middle of the pitch ready to call the captains to order and commence proceedings. It works, and a player from each side approaches just as Cyril said they would. It's a doddle this refereeing!

Preliminaries over and we are off. Got to run the diagonal, opposite corners to my club linesmen. Must get my bearings, which corners are the linesmen covering? Oh hell, they're both on the same side of the pitch! Ball goes out of play and I go over and redirect the nearest to the other side with my apologies. He's not impressed.

Do I blow every time the ball goes out for a throw-in or goal kick or not? A simple practical application like when to blow the whistle had never been covered in Cyril's front parlour. I decide to blow for everything but I get fed up of hearing it about ten minutes after all the players did. I'll change that routine in the second half.

Game continues and the stronger visiting side start notching up the goals. Playing uphill they've moved into a five goal lead when I hear a despairing call from the touchline, "How much longer you goin' to play this 'arf ref?" What does he mean, how much longer? I look at my watch, we've played 52 minutes - the under-17s only play 40 minutes each way! Oh hell, another cock-up. I play a few more seconds before authoritatively bringing the half to a belated end.

Second half is uneventful with the Scunthorpe side running out 12-1 victors. The home side are knackered but I reason that the experience of playing in their first 90 minute game will serve them well for the future. They dutifully pay me with a flippant aside that I'll get no overtime payment today. It's over, I've survived. The offer of a lift back to town with the visitors is too good to miss, although I can hear Cyril's warning about such practices ringing in my ears as I climb into the back of a Reliant Robin van with five team members.

I referee for a further four months before retiring. I know that I wasn't very good at it, a view shared by each team whose weekend's activity I blighted. The option to play the game on a regular basis offered an escape route I was quick to seize. But my refereeing experience helped me to associate with future match officials and as I moved upwards in playing terms I became more appreciative of good referees and less tolerant of poor ones.

Twenty-seven years later I re-qualify to become a referee. Same procedure, learning in someone's front room, the same verbal and written exam and a similar success but with an improved mark. It's been a long time coming but I really do enjoy my refereeing now. My earliest experiences make me look at some of the young lads taking up refereeing nowadays and I know they have a much harder time in staying the course than someone entering the calling later in life. Those that stay the distance deserve the support and respect of all their fellow members.

3 - The Day I Ref'd in Broadmoor and Escaped to Tell the Tale

The totally true story of one of my very early match fixtures

It was an innocent enough looking fixture tucked amongst my October list, Patmoor Strikers v Britwell Chicken Ranch Reserves, East Berkshire League Division 6. Turning to the handbook for the club details caused a short intake of breath. Patmoor Strikers home ground was Broadmoor Hospital. Colours black and red stripes, black shorts, special note: all fixtures home and away will be played at the hospital. Yes, that's the Broadmoor, special secure hospital for the criminally insane. Now for the first time I feel secure enough to relate how I refereed at Broadmoor and escaped to tell the tale.

It was late October 1994; I'd only qualified as a referee for the second time in February of the same year and had just started my first full season. Things had been going pretty well and I'd been confident enough to submit an application for promotion. But Broadmoor! How could they do this to me at this early stage in my refereeing career?

I looked in the local footballer's gospel, The Maidenhead Advertiser, for the latest league tables and saw that Patmoor Strikers were next to bottom with their visitors holding down a mid-table position. Patmoor Strikers (Pat for PATients, moor for BroadMOOR, best not think too much about the Strikers bit I decided) had gained just one point from five league games played to date.

The procedure in the East Berkshire League is that the home team contact the match referee to confirm the fixture and arrangements at least four days prior to the match. The phone duly went on the Tuesday evening. P.E. Instructor Humphries introduced himself, confirmed the fixture and asked if I'd been to Broadmoor previously. I was quick to inform him that I hadn't, as a referee or in any other capacity.

I was told to report to the main entrance 45 minutes prior to kick-off where, along with the visiting team, I would be met and escorted through the grounds to the pitch. "You may get a phone call on the morning of the match if it's misty. We like to be able to see them all and we are worried about our right winger. "Out of sight and he'll likely make a dash for the wall" added P.E.I. Humphries. He's only worried about the right winger; I'm worried about all the team, subs and spectators. Still at least there was a lifeline, perhaps it will be foggy on the day, after all it is late October.

Hopes are raised and then quashed as the fateful day duly arrives. A beautifully sunny autumn day. I'm resigned to fulfilling the fixture and am determined to enjoy the experience and treat the game as just another Saturday afternoon run-out. I make the 15-mile trip to Crowthorne, a pleasant Berkshire village; follow the signs to the hospital; meander through winding streets bordered by obvious staff residences and then it meets you. Thirty-foot high brick walls topped with barbwire. 'This is Broadmoor Hospital' the sign greets you. More signs direct you to the car park and then on to the main reception.

I'm told to wait in the holding area until the visiting team turns up. Perhaps they won't fulfil the fixture. No chance, a party of 14 carrying kitbags and footballs approach. My fate is finally sealed; I'm going inside! We all have to pass through a metal detecting archway, bags are searched separately and the uniformed guard takes great delight in dismantling my linesmen's flags to make sure that I'm not smuggling in some banned substance in the handles.

We pass through a courtyard, entering another building, down a corridor where a notice board catches my eye and one notice in particular - Halloween Disco this Saturday 5pm to 8pm. Do the patients really have to keep junior school hours?

Through another door on to the outside, through a sector control gateway and then two more control points. The perimeter wall is in view and nestled at the bottom of the gentle incline is the pitch. A good flat surface. A small grandstand is already filling up with the sunshine attracting the casual supporters as well as those taking the opportunity to wander around the touchline in gentle exercise.

We are ushered into one of two sports pavilions to change. For the first time I notice the visiting team. Apart from one old hand they all look under twenty. Do they really understand the impending potential danger they are in? Do they appreciate how one silly act of retaliation could be their last? I don't think that one of them thought for one minute about the consequences on my future refereeing career or very existence. How totally inconsiderate the youth of today is.

We're all changed, out we go. There's a good crowd gathered now. Next to the pitch is a cricket field complete with clock-crested pavilion, separate scoreboard and seats dotted around the boundary. You could hardly imagine a more English setting, and then you remember the walls.

The home team is kicking in towards one of the goals when suddenly I see him! All dressed in black, stood in the centre circle, another referee! The mind works overtime. It must be a cock-up on arrangements; they've appointed two refs. I might yet be saved from this fate worse than death at the very last moment. I offer up thanks to the Patron Saint of Referees (St. Jeff the Ref?).

I march on to the centre circle and greet my qualified colleague. "Hello" he says, "I'm Lennie, Patmoor Strikers club linesman". I can't take it in. He answers my unasked question. "I qualified before I came in here, there are three of us resident here, we take it in turn to run the line". St Jeff how could you do this to me - a nutter on the line!

After the preliminaries I eventually get the game underway. I look around for potential flashpoints. There's a man-mountain at centre half for the Strikers - 6.9" at least, tattoos, scars, bandaged knees and as broad as any guardhouse door. The Chicken Ranchers frontline all appear to be ten-second 100-yarders. Man-mountain can't hope to contain them fairly. It can only be a matter of time before I have to make some serious decisions about my future!

One crumb of comfort amongst all my terror-stricken thoughts although I'm up for promotion there's hardly likely to be an assessor present today and so if some of my decisions are not so good then only the biased view of Britwell Chicken Ranch Reserves will be witness to it. Then six minutes into the game man-mountain falls and hurts his back. He has to be substituted (St. Jeff is obviously back on duty).

Half-time arrives without further incident or goals. This is mainly due to the acrobatics of the Patmoor keeper, a black lad who is keeping the visitors at bay almost single-handed.

Lennie has been doing a good job too. The Berks & Bucks F.A. encourage full participation from club linesmen and Lennie has been scrupulously fair in his application of the offside law. He takes me under his wing at half-time, shares his orange juice with me and enters into general discussion about the game so far. I comment on the keeper. "Used to be on Brentford's books," says Lennie. A supporter (sorry patient) wandering along the touchline shouts across "Lennie the Blues are winning 1-0". "I'm a Chelsea fan" he explains. "I murdered my wife you know" he continued without drawing breath. If you are ever looking for a conversation stopper try that line, it certainly put me back momentarily. "Time we were getting this second half underway" I stammered, ignoring his confession whilst turning and quickly distancing myself from him.

Midway through the second half and the visitors finally get past the former Bee to take the lead. A perfectly good goal, no controversy - thank you St. Jeff. The Strikers rouse themselves to respond but they really aren't good enough. However, a deflected long-range effort loops over the visiting keeper into the back of the net to draw them level and boy do they celebrate. Half the team go into the grandstand to hug their supporters, dancing on the touchline and 'high-fives' all round. There had been a F.A. directive that referees should curtail any lengthy celebrations. Would you voluntarily go into a crowd of 200 convicted insane murderers to reprimand them for over celebrating - no, neither did I.

Party over and the game continues drifting into a drawn conclusion. The Strikers are happy, they've recorded their second goal and second league point of the season. The visitors trudge off disappointed that their dominance hasn't been translated into points. The ref is very relieved. I shake hands with both linesmen and Lennie the Lino wants to talk some more and in my relaxed state, who am I to stop him? He queries a couple of decisions that I am happy to discuss and clarify with him. "We had a riot here last game," he says. "Lost one-nil to a goal pushed in by a hand. "Neither me or the ref could see in the crowded goalmouth. "Four of the team can't play any more this season as punishment for what went on then." "I murdered my two kids as well you know" he dropped almost matter-of-fact into the conversation. "How did the Blues end up" I piped up in an attempt to distract him from confessing any further. If he did reply I didn't hear him as I burst into a short sprint to the sanctuary of the dressing room.

Marched back through the complex, collected my match fee from the main reception and safely back in my car. Time to catch up with all the results coming through on the radio. 'Arsenal 1 Ipswich 0, Chelsea 1 Blackburn 4'. At the mention of Chelsea I tense up, casting a nervous glance over my shoulder just to make sure that Lennie hadn't stowed away somehow and was escaping via the back seat of my car. All clear.

I wonder what other stories I might have heard if I'd stopped around to hear Lennie's answer. Best not to think about it too much, but even today I can't hear the Chelsea result without having to look behind me and wondering if Lennie the Lino has confided in another referee today.

------- oooOooo ------

4 - I Knew It Was Going To Be A Bad Game When

You know as soon as you get up some days that everything is not going to work out very well. Refereeing football matches can be like that.

I knew it was going to be a bad game when the home club Treasurer greeted me with "How much do you think you are worth today then ref?" I took this as an invite to lodge my costs and replied "£10 match fee and £3.60 mileage." His response was immediate and cutting, "Good flight was it?"

Well I know the expenses equalled a thirty-mile round trip and it was a bit further than the usual Sunday morning game but it was a County Cup appointment after all. And I was really looking forward to it. Since moving to Huddersfield I've come to terms with the absence of flat pitches but having to travel twenty miles to find a bit of flat ground to check the oil level in the car is a bit much. That's why this game offered me a good chance to check the car fluids whilst getting paid for the mileage as well. I could well do without the treasurer's biting wit which set the tone of the day.

Have you ever had one of those games when you are convinced that the club linesman is the village idiot? His sole purpose in life is to offer his weekly services to the local team every Sunday morning and then go on to provide amusement to all with his frantic flag waving antics which bear very little resemblance to anything happening on the pitch. Then when you really want him his head is down and he is having a conversation with a buttercup he's happened upon.

Playing one man short throughout infuriated one mature spectator who repeatedly pleaded with the team manager to give him a shirt and let him on at 'em. It was explained to me later that they dare not risk playing this accident prone geriatric as, in the words of the club secretary, "It would cause insurance complications!"

Football is incidental to the main purpose of this club which used sport as an excuse for a good social life. Nothing wrong with that. Shouting at the ref is just their way of building up a thirst for the main event in the clubhouse afterwards. It's the type of club that when it receives a grant from the National Playing Fields Association, decides to spend it on extending the bar!

Players in this sort of team are not often there for their passing ability or aerial prowess, it's who they sup with and how much beer they buy for the manager that keeps them in the team. Failing that they have to have some special talent, not necessarily football related. One particular player in this team certainly had that. A fairly meaty full back who was deaf and dumb who communicated by loud honking noises and strange gestures which struck terror into his opponents. It was certainly intimidating but nothing I felt I was in a position to do anything about.

Not the best of days but at least I now know that the oil level in the car is okay for another couple of weeks.

------- oooOooo ------

5 - How To Drop The Referee In The Fertiliser

Guidance for ambitious linesmen - sorry Assistant Referees

On the long haul to the top of the ladder of success for referees there comes a time when you are more frequently an Assistant Referee rather than the Referee in charge. It's during this period that you grow to respect or hate the bastard in black - sorry, senior official in the middle.

Most weekends you know that you are ten times better than your senior colleague and the fact that he keeps disregarding your signals is making everything so much worse. You can't believe that this jerk has got further than you have and worse than that he is likely to progress ahead of you and so slow down your own rate of promotion.

So what can you do about it? Well you can certainly reduce his effectiveness in this match, which may lead to a drop in his overall confidence and eventually to a reduction in his status. But you have to be careful about it. You need to drop him in it without drawing the assessors attention to your own performance. So when you need to take advantage of such an opportunity then you need to follow the *'Thirteen Steps to Dropping Your Referee in the Fertiliser!'*

1. Raise the flag to indicate a foul then change hands and point the other way when the referee (who has now blown) could have played an advantage.

2. Indicate a goal kick when it is obviously a corner (or vice versa) and the referee has a better view.

3. When the referee obviously needs help from you, ensure you don't look at him.

4. Call the referee across to report an incident where disciplinary action needs to be taken, and then fail to identify the culprit.

5. Flag for an incident right underneath the referee's nose.

6. Have a player cautioned or sent off when you're not really sure he should be.

7. When the referee asks for a time check make sure you knock five minutes off the time remaining.

8. Get involved with the game unnecessarily.

9. Fail to indicate the ball is out of play and the team goes on and scores.

10. Flag to the referee's back.

11. Talk 'out of turn' when it would be better for the referee to be taking charge of a situation (especially when dealing with managers).

12. Indicate off-side too quickly, when the player concerned is not really interfering with play and a screaming 35 yard shot is disallowed.

13. Fail to report a major incident to the referee that he has not seen.

The referee will of course be wise to most of these tricks having made the same progress himself and will be armed ready to counter all your moves and have a few aggressive ones of his own. Don't be riled by him referring to you the Referee's assistant but quietly remind him that in fact you are the Assistant Referee, an important member of his team and don't let him forget it.

------- oooOooo ------

6 - The Craic In The Changing Room

For referees who have been players, the craic in the dressing room is the thing that is most missed. But some Saturdays it re-appears.

Even in the professional game players will talk of 'The Craic' they have in the club. There is no other word to describe it. It's the camaraderie, team spirit, good-natured leg-pulling - it's The Craic. And once you are no longer part of the team it's the thing you remember and miss most. The time you all pulled a fast one on the manager by not turning up at the pre-arranged place prior to a game, then when he arrived at the changing rooms all-a-bother, there you all were, stripped and ready to go. Hiding your team-mates clothes, pouring washing up liquid in his shoes, all the stupid things you wouldn't dare do anywhere else. It's the jokes you play on each other, it's the banter, it's The Craic, there is no other word for it.

So when you become a referee in the local park league you are external to all this. With the push to provide separate changing accommodation for match officials the chances to revisit your youth are rapidly diminishing. But just occasionally you end up in some location which hasn't quite caught up with the League's best intentions yet and you have to share changing accommodation with one or both of the teams. Last season I had a few such occasions and I wasn't disappointed to discover that The Craic lives on. Still as crude as ever, so I apologise for repeating some of the tales which as always balance towards the toilet side of humour, which, at my age, I am supposed to be above. I'm pleased to report that I'm not.

There was the team captain holding his team talk prior to kick-off sat on the toilet with door opened wide on to the changing room. Like the King addressing his people he just sat on his throne shouting out team orders to the accompanying sounds of his bowels being evacuated.

Then there is the talk of sex of course, never far away from the top of any team's agenda. One disillusioned player thought that sex was overplayed. "You can get as much pleasure out of a good shit as you can out of having your leg-over" he proclaimed. A few disbelieving heads shook around the room until one team-mate suggested that he must be doing one of them wrong but didn't venture any further in suggesting which it might be.

A player was recounting his vasectomy operation to the captive audience getting changed for a league game. All the gory details you would expect but the piece that caught my imagination came at the end when he told of the testing process to make sure that he really was firing blanks.

"You have to give two all-clear samples a couple of weeks apart before you can climb on in total safety" he explained. "By the time it came to give the second I was really getting frustrated at the delays in testing out my enhanced tackle. So, when the Doc gave me a bottle and told me to take it home and ejaculate into it, I decided to take matters into my own hands there and then. I went behind his curtain and got straight on with the job. Within two minutes I had handed him a steaming sample to be proud of. You should have seen his face as his hand curled around the warm glass tube."

------- oooOooo ------

7 - A Game of Two Halves

Normally a game of two halves refers to a single football match whereas on this occasion we are talking about the two halves of the country.

They frequently say that 'Football is a game of two halves' to reflect the differences you often witness during a single match. I want to take it a little further and suggest to you that park football in England is very different in the north of England to the south. A game of two halves of the country.

Having refereed in four different areas in the country I like to think that I can speak with some authority on the matter. Two years in North Lincolnshire, the next two years in Maidenhead followed by six years in Huddersfield and now into my second season in Aylesbury

I'm not suggesting that one is better than the other, they are just different, both have their good and bad points and I've enjoyed the differences they offer.

Let's start with the weather, that most basic of English interests, which can affect any sport. In my four years in the south I've never had to call a game off because of the weather. My games have been called off before I've got anywhere near looking at the pitch, usually days in advance of the game. In fact I've never got as near as doing a pitch inspection to see if a game can start. Yet in the north it's almost a weekly occurrence during the winter months, especially on a Sunday morning following a stiff frost or overnight snow.

Being high up in the Pennines meant that very few pitches were on a true level, you were more likely to be needing rope and tackle to run a true diagonal on the 1 in 7's that dominate the West Yorkshire leagues. Playing on the side of a mountain can be a bugger on the knees especially when the wind decides to blow, which is most weeks.

In the four years that I've officiated in the south it's never been cold enough for me to resort to wearing a long sleeved uniform. Yet in the north I couldn't have survived without one and a thermal vest underneath some weeks. I have to confess that Father Christmas once brought me some black finger-less gloves specifically for some added protection on the colder Sunday mornings although I have to say that I never did get the nerve to wear them. It's bad enough winning over the players in Yorkshire without dressing up in bus-conductors (remember them?) attire.

That brings me on to the relationship between players and referees, and the differences I've noted around the country. Without doubt referees in Aylesbury are treated with more respect than anywhere else I've ref'd in the country. In the main I've been warmly greeted, made welcome, been treated as a normal human being, frequently paid before kick-off and generally regarded as good for the game and your decisions are accepted at face value and your mistakes tolerated with bemusement or only mild abuse.

Now in Yorkshire your real purpose in being there is often to stop players killing each other! Huddersfield is the most sport orientated town I've come across - football, rugby league, cricket, they are fanatical about them all. The local Saturday league has 14 divisions and a similar number on Sundays and there are never enough referees to staff all the games. Yet players still treat you with total disdain, often ignoring your very presence until you aggravate them with a decision against them. But then after the game the mood totally changes, you are always invited back to the pub for food and banter, the game is over and you are very much part of the after match post mortem discussions.

Huddersfield has a high ethnic population and that brings intense rivalry and racist tensions which referees have to be aware of, and deal with.

Facilities in the Aylesbury area far outweigh those in the north. Maybe it's because of the high number of games played every week in Huddersfield but school pitches are in high demand and that means everyone, including the ref, getting changed in large cloakrooms. Very rarely do you get separate changing accommodation but at least school facilities mean that you are likely to have an after-match shower, not something you can rely on in most other places.

I have to admit to a soft spot for Aylesbury football as it allowed me to referee my first international game - (The) New Zealand (a local boozer) v Brazil70 (a gang of lads of high aspirations and low ability). Now that would never have happened in Huddersfield.

Maybe I'm softening up but I was almost tempted to slip my thermal vest into the kit bag the other week, probably the age factor, perhaps I'll write about that next time. Football really is a game of two halves. Viva la difference!

------- oooOooo ------

8 - Diary of a Referee's Season

Well half a season actually but we are not being picky cos refs aren't, are they?

After moving from Huddersfield to Aylesbury I found myself writing letters back to Yorkshire for printing in the Referee's Association monthly magazine. This was primarily for my benefit as the letters will explain.

September Letter

I know that you couldn't give a toss about me moving 'darn sarf' but I have to talk to someone about refereeing south of Watford Gap, so just sit still and listen for once will you. It's very different to the hills of Huddersfield so I thought you might act as my therapist to help me ease into the rigours of a different world, although it is still local football this is the Berks & Bucks County F.A. and the Aylesbury District League. Let me recount my early days of the season just to show you how different it is.

My first game in the area, no friendlies in preparation, and straight into the Aylesbury Sunday Combination League 1st Division. I'm at the Aylesbury equivalent of Leeds Road but here there are just 5 pitches. I arrive an hour before kick-off time on a Sunday morning but already most of the teams are here. Pitch inspection reveals an excellent covering of grass, no dog-shit, no glass, no condoms and all line markings good and clear. Nets and flags already put up by Council staff. Match fee is £20 and it is paid before kick-off in line with League rules, now that is a good idea.

Linesmen get their instructions cos here they do off-sides and much more, and then we are off. What a crap match, it's supposed to be Division 1 but the standard resembles Huddersfield Sunday League Division 4. And everyone is so dam friendly to each other, they really don't need a ref. I book a couple of players controversially to try and liven things up a bit but to no avail. I can't believe it is always going to be this easy, hope not anyway.

I'm off to Long Marston this Saturday where we get changed in the village hall. Pitch has lots of grass and is flat, very flat. Very different to the one-in-sevens of Huddersfield. Much better match this, more competitive, two bookings and 4-3 to the visitors and we all had a good game. In fact that's the problem, everyone is so dam friendly, to me and to each other. This sort of behaviour is going to get football a good name. Surely it can't always be like this - please!

Sunday morning for a village derby second division game. Three reds, five yellers - this is more like it, now I'm earning my corn. One of the sending-offs is based on a club linesman's sayso. He's an active Class 5 referee and sees an off the ball headbutt which results in the player protesting his innocence but still walking. Not sure if I've done the right thing here and I decide that I will never again send a player off based solely on a linesman's sayso.

Still we had a good game, 5-3 to the visitors and despite all the colourful cards I waved around I'm still well received by both teams. In three games I've issued three reds and nine yellows and not one of those was for dissent - I've decided that Berks & Bucks must be a dissent free zone. That would be nice.

The monthly meeting of the Aylesbury R.A. is graced by mine and Premiership referee Graham Barber's attendance. Graham is one of two Premiership refs living in the area - the other is Graham Poll. The R.A. membership is only 50 but 32 of them are there on this night. If only Huddersfield could get a 64% turn-out. Maybe it's the Monday evening date that attracts them. Amongst the membership are four women, including the R.A. Treasurer, and three lads under 16. That's got to be healthy. Graham Barber's talk on tactical refereeing is excellent. Don't bother going deep and wide he said, it's a waste of time because you just get yourself caught out of position - did you hear that Neil?

Another village game as I move up into the Premier Division. Another super flat and grassy pitch and another good game - just one booking and everyone is still happy and friendly. If I had been treated like this in Huddersfield I would have feared for my car or something worse! One thing I have noticed is that you don't get invited back to the club after the game for pie and peas and a beer. Wonder why?

I was really looking forward to my well-earned early season break. After only a handful of games I'm due a first break of the year, one which has seen me move from the homeliness of West Yorkshire to the unfamiliar setting of Buckinghamshire. Moving home and job is always a stressful time especially moving into an area where you don't know a soul and Mary and I were both well ready for the planned 12 days in Lanzarote which beckons after a final two-game weekend.

You will recognise that some games in which you referee that the players are of very limited ability especially when you get into the lower divisions of the local leagues. My two games this weekend both fell into this category. That's never a problem for me as I know that these lads enjoy their game just as much as those performing at a higher level and take it just as seriously.

My Saturday game followed that model. As I did my pre-match pitch inspection I was met by a neighbouring householder who complained about the language that all neighbours suffered each weekend emanating from the sports ground. I also noted a nearby playground well populated on this pleasant Saturday afternoon. So I gave a stronger message than usual about bad language to the team captains and, would you believe it, I never had a problem all game.

Both teams took the game very seriously and a close 2-1 victory for the visitors kept all interested throughout the 90 minutes. My northern accent again drew enquiries and cheeky banter but all good-natured. A first card-free game of the season and we all enjoyed ourselves, even the neighbours I suspect.

Sunday was very different, a game totally devoid of skill, few showing any committed effort and a farcical 11-5 score-line. What a joke! And that's just how both teams treated it - a game for a larf! If I could have booked players for not taking the game seriously I certainly would have done and had a bookful as well. Such was the casual manner of the whole game that there wasn't a serious tackle all game and no chance for me to take out my frustrations on any of the players by flourishing a couple of yellers!

There was actually one outrageous display of skill which drew applause from players on both sides and a surprisingly high number of spectators. The home keeper picked the ball out of his net for the tenth time, took one almighty kick out of his hands, launching into orbit back towards the centre-spot. Coming from out a sun-filled sky to be caught on the left instep and dropped dead-still on the centre-spot by the referee (moi). Sod it I'm off to the sun.

CARD COUNT   Games 9   Yellers 16   Reds 3

October Letter

First day back in Blighty and there is a Aylesbury R.A. meeting, the second Monday of each month, and the guest speaker is a 21 year-old midfielder with Aylesbury United. 'The Ducks' play in the Ryeman League (similar standard to Emley) and Ollie spoke about life as a failed YTS with Northampton Town and his aspirations still to become a professional footballer. He talked about the commitment that semi-pros have to enter into, the rewards, the difficulties and his views on referees. For a young lad he was very articulate and with a 50% turn-out of membership it was again an enjoyable evening.

Back from the sun and a tan to show off but little else to look back on with two straight-forward but enjoyable games, two yellers and I get very wet for the first time this season. The right knee has stiffened up a bit after games this season and even the sun break hasn't eased it at all.

Two straightforward matches and one moment that tickled me. It came

BASTARD IN BLACK

on the Saturday, the home centre-forward was a big black lad. For the third time he went through one-on-one with the keeper and for the third time he lifted his shot wide. I was jogging (yes jogging) back into position with him after his latest miss when a wag from the touch-line shouted "You big useless black bastard". Without a second thought my new Caribbean friend turned to me and said "They're talking about you ref!"

The standards set for changing accommodation in the local league could be of interest to you as I remember the HRA attempts to improve facilities of last season. The three-division Sunday League stipulates that Division One sides must have suitable changing room and washing facilities; Division Two sides must have a suitable changing room and there are no minimum standards for Division Three teams.

I told you a couple of months ago about sending a player off on the say-so of a club linesman. Linesmen play a bigger role in the Berks & Bucks area and give off-sides etc not at all like their West Riding counterparts. On this occasion I had an active Class 5 referee on one line and he saw a head-butt which I acted on. Now the player has appealed against the sending-off and that hearing will be heard shortly but before then I've got a couple of games to get through.

A couple of good games in the weekend sunshine, four yellers and one amusing incident when I booked a guy called Oliver Kolodziejsm. Struggling to get the spelling right, I handed the notebook over to the culprit and he completed the paperwork for me. I'm sure the instructors wouldn't have approved but it certainly was appreciated by many.

Sunday was a third division fixture on a local park pitch. The players are spoilt down here. The nets and flags are all fixed in position by Council staff and taken down by them at the end of the game, the pitches are flat and have plenty of grass on them and there has obviously been some repair work down on them during the close season. Not like Huddersfield at all. I checked my kit bag before setting off. Two whistles, two pencils, flags, notebook, tie-ups, padlock and key.....padlock and key!?! Yes it's an essential part of any referees equipment for Council pitches in the Aylesbury area. Referees are invited to secure their own changing room with their own padlock. All the Council pitches have separate officials changing rooms with separate toilets and showers - bliss!

CARD COUNT   Games = 13   Yellers = 21   Reds = 3   Card Free Games = 4

November Letter

Friday night and the County F.A. Appeal Hearing is to be held in a Buckingham hotel about 15 miles from where I live. The Berks & Bucks County HQ is in Oxfordshire (don't ask!) and they travel around the County for disciplinary hearings and appeals. Arriving in good time to mingle with guests for a Murder Mystery Dinner before spotting an obvious F.A. official - blazer, blue tie with badge, clipboard - and I make myself known. The player appears late but eventually we get going.

He immediately questions my right to send him off solely on the word of a club linesman. He gets short shrift from the chair of the panel who informs him that I had acted entirely correctly as the linesman, even a club linesman, is the representative of the F.A. for those 90 minutes. That pleased me as I wasn't sure if I had been right or not.

However the lad has two witnesses, one of them being the opponent he had supposedly head-butted. It's obvious my club linesman had made a mistake (and that's being kind) and in the absence of a written report from him the case is 'Not Proven'. I'm not unduly worried about the decision going against me, just pleased that I had been right in acting on the linesman's observations.

Saturday morning get notification of a Sunday County Cup appointment, so that's a good start to the weekend. Out in a small village for a Aylesbury District League game and a good contest ends 3-3, everyone happy and no cards. Back into Aylesbury for a Sunday game on another flat, grassy Council pitch. Again the teams are very moderate but they are taking it seriously and thoroughly enjoy themselves with the home side coming out on top by 3-1. The ref keeps his cards in his pocket to complete a card-free weekend. However I pull a thigh muscle late in the first half and only just manage to complete the game. It tightens up later and I already know that I wont be reffing next weekend. Hope it clears up for my County Cup debut on the 25th.

Last month I told you that I was suffering with a pulled muscle and this kept me out of the game for three weeks. Weekends aren't the same without a game to be involved in but I take the opportunity to watch a few games in the area. Aylesbury United ('The Ducks' - Aylesbury Duck get it?) are the nearest club and they are having a good season in the first division of the Ryeman League. I reckon to watch their mid-week games so decide to give them a miss on my first free Saturday and venture out to visit the new Oxford United ground when they entertain Cheltenham Town in what is a labelled a 'Derby' game.

It's nice enough but like so many of the new grounds its all breeze-blocks and plastic, expensive as well at £20 for an upper-tier seat. Up there you have the added advantage of being able to watch your car in the car-park. With one end without a stand at all (early McAlpine manner) you can stand watch over your own motor.

I return to action with a Sunday League game with the home team's run of wins being halted in a 3-3 draw and my thigh muscle goes again. I'm going to have to rest it again.

The November R.A. meeting welcomes a referee from the RAF and he tells us about his life which appears to revolve around reffing three games a week in different parts of the country. He is a PE Instructor and runs teams in the national services league. So when his teams are not playing he is reffing. That means most days he is almost always involved in a football match in some capacity. Rough life in the forces aint it? Guest speakers get presented with a bottle of wine by way of a thank you, not a patch on the Society tie is it?

Members are informed that next month John Baker, Ken Ridden's successor as the FA Head of Referees, will be our guest. We are also told that he is not a good speaker but an important man in refereeing circles. Sounds inviting doesn't it. The meeting closed exactly at 10pm as it always does. Regardless of what doesn't get included, come hell or high water, we are all on our way by 10.

In preparation for my return to the middle after the injury I've invested in some black cycling shorts to wear under my uniform in the hope that they will provide some warmth and insurance against a re-occurrence of the muscle pull. I'm sure Don wouldn't have approved of such deviation from regulation gear but I always was a disappointment to him, as I suspect many of us were but the trouble was that he would judge us by his own high standards which most of us were never likely to achieve.

December Letter

It's New Years Day morning as I sit down to pen this month's update on my missionary work down south and, as in so many things, its a time to reflect and also look forward with renewed optimism. Today offers a chance to re-establish my links with Huddersfield as I'm off to watch the Terriers this afternoon when they visit Wycombe Wanderers. High Wycombe is about 30 miles from my home, the Adams Park ground is one I know well having been a regular visitor during my earlier time in this area when I lived in Maidenhead for two years. Luton and Watford are the nearest League grounds to my current home but I've still to visit either.

On the refereeing front I've had my first game cancelled because of the weather. An overnight frost means the Sunday morning fixture wont go ahead but it's not my decision. I get a 9am phone call from the home team telling me the game is off. Not sure who has called it off, home team or Council but I do know it's deprived me of my £10 attendance fee. Referees are entitled to half their match fee if attending when the game is off, bit different to Huddersfield where you only get expenses.

The cycling shorts I bought last month are doing the business and I've had no more problems with the thigh muscle so managed to get a full complement of games in over the month. Ventured out of the County into Bedfordshire last week to take a game in Bletchley, older members will know the importance of Bletchley as the centre for war time code breakers and there is still a museum devoted to the art in the town to this day. Although cold I'm still wearing a short-sleeved referee's shirt which makes me a bit of a novelty down here where most of the players have been playing in gloves for several weeks now. I don't half give 'em some stick - southern softies!

For the first time I have to get changed with one of the teams. Every match previously had seen me having separate changing facilities, again very different to Huddersfield. The match is without incident and I've now gone five games without issuing a card of any sort. At the November RA meeting I'm informed that during September and October I issued more cards than any other referee in the Aylesbury area. The County FA publish refereeing league tables based on cards shown and circulate to appointment secretaries. I aint going to remain at the top (or should it be bottom?) for very long on current form.

My first game of the year is to be a County Cup appointment which appeared out of the blue. Last sixteen of the Saturday competition, Newport Pagnell Town v Wing Village under floodlights with two appointed assistants. I haven't officiated in any County competition down here before and have only done local leagues in the Aylesbury area so was a bit taken back by this appointment. Can only think it's going to be a sixteen - nil outcome but the recognition is very welcome and I'm looking forward to it.

The December RA meeting has John Baker, FA Head of Referees, as guest speaker and despite his reputation for being a poor speaker he gives a good presentation ably assisted by an excellent FA video with discussion spots on the styles of top referees - very revealing. Graham Poll is classed as a chatterbox, taking every opportunity to talk to players during a game. Mark Clattenburg is probably the today equivilant and we all know what problems he's landed in by talking to players. It used to be seen as an important tool in the ref's armoury if you could keep players 'on-side' with a few words of wisdom noe and a again but nowadays anything you say to a player is high risk and likely to come back to bite you.

The Aylesbury RA has a long-standing magazine editor who produces a monthly eight-page colour issue. There are only two ways to receive your copy, either via email (and around half the membership now get it this way) or by attending the monthly meeting. I haven't contributed anything to it yet but will have to dig into my catalogue of past articles built up over the four years as your magazine editor to offer him something soon. Trouble is, that once you show an interest then you never know what it might lead to, and before long you are you are arguing in print with the national executive (again!) and bang goes the new year resolution.

It seems that I ran out of steam here and there are no records of letters for the rest of that season. Wish I was better at keeping records altogether. Sometimes I wonder how many matches I have referee'd over the years? I know that it is not as many as games I have played in and for all the enjoyment I get in officiating you can't beat playing the game.

------- oooOooo ------

9 - The Old Farts League Rules

These Senior Leagues are sometimes also known as 'Master's League', 'Veteran's League', 'Over-30's League', "Old Farts League", "'Hey, look at them Old Guys trying to play football' League"

When you progress to playing senior league football games tend to operate to a different set of rules, Here you get a sample of some of the more popular rules for 'The Old Farts League'.

1. Teams shall consist of more than 11 players on the day before the match, but less than 11 on the day of the match. If by bad management a team should have more than 11 players at kick-off time then all present players shall be allowed to start the game in the sure knowledge that some will soon be injured and numbers reduced.

2. No team shall possess its own kit. If they do, it must be old and dingy. Perhaps even smelly.

3. If the kit is borrowed there shall be no more than eight matching shirts.

4. Not more than any three players shall wear the same colour socks and there shall be at least three different colours of shirts worn.

5. If the local pub has afternoon closing, the kick-off time and length of match shall be arranged such that the pub will be open at the end of said match.

6. No match shall have a qualified referee, nor any linesman, assigned. If a qualified referee shows up he must know nothing about the offside rule.

7. A team captain's only function shall be to take part in the coin toss-up (if there is one). No footballing ability is necessary or desirable.

8. Teams shall be permitted to use ringers, but it must be understood that each ringer playing for a team in one match shall be permitted to play against that team in the next. All ringers shall be identified on the team-sheet by using the secretary's name.

9. Each team shall laugh uncontrollably at any mis-kick, own goal, etc.

Any team not following this rule will be deemed to be taking the game too seriously and shall not be asked to play again.

10. No player shall intentionally foul an opponent, but unintentional fouls caused by ineptitude shall be permissible. Any such fouls will be ignored by the referee as long as the offender helps the fouled player to his feet whilst not pinching his arm.

11. Each team shall have a special player. This will be ageing former ball-player who can no longer run to save his life. He shall be stuck out on the wing and shall take all throw-ins, corners and free kicks but otherwise shall take no part in the game apart from berating his team-mates for refusing to pass the ball to him.

12. After the match both teams shall meet in the pub, but each team shall nominate a player who cannot attend because he has to meet his significant other half.

Otherwise all the usual rules of football shall apply, except with the mutual agreement of both teams and the referee (if there is one). ☺

------- oooOooo ------

10 - In Defence of the Referee

The 'Bastard in Black Award for Jounalistic Services to Refereeing' goes to Michael Parkinson for this article first published in The Daily Telegraph.

In the culture of buck passing and prevarication in football it is either the media or the referee to blame for everything. Arsene Wenger thinks the time has come for video evidence to be allowed to assist the officials. Anyone who has heard the Arsenal manager claiming he didn't see the incident when one of his players misbehaved on the field will know his eyesight isn't what it should be and sympathise with someone so visually impaired as to need video evidence for that which most of us can see quite clearly with the naked eye.

His is a common complaint among football managers who have eyes of a sparrowhawk in their opponent's penalty area but are afflicted with a terrible myopia in their own half of the field.

Which is why you might imagine they would be more sympathetic to blind referees. Not a bit of it. Chelsea's Gianluca Vialli says referees have got it in for Denis Wise. Diddums. Ian Wright is a marked man, a victim. David Batty is a pussy cat really. Bonny Lad. It's the referees to blame for all the bookings. There ought to be two of them, one in each half of the pitch. Why stop there? Why not one for each player? Plus video evidence. That should do the trick.

The other suggestion is whether there should be one referee on the field or 22 they should be drawn from the ranks of ex-players. They know what's what. It would be a bit like putting a wife beater in charge of a marriage bureau.

Why anyone would want to be a referee nowadays beats me. They are reviled, spat upon, cursed, terrorised, jostled and threatened. And that's what happens when they come through the junior leagues. When they reach the top of their profession things get much worse. For what? The kind of money the modern player would consider to be loose change. They must be crackers. What is more they are isolated in their misery. The F.A. do nothing, which is what the F.A. do better than most. They are much too busy bothering about the opinions of Senor Havelange and whither Wembley, which only reveals their enthusiasm for lost causes. Both are monuments to the game's past and, in my view, have nothing to do with the future. The same could be said, of course, about the F.A.

Why should Wembley be so important to us securing a future World Cup? It might be the most famous football ground in the world but it's a long way from being the best. As it is any claim we have for the future will depend not on what happens to Wembley but what happens in France. Any trouble with our hooligans and Borneo would have a better chance of playing host.

How do we change the ugly faces on the terraces? Changing the ugly faces on the field and on the bench would be a start. No one wants the game to lose its cutting edge but managers and players must begin to accept responsibility for what happens on the field of play. Blind referees have nothing to do with it. In the final analysis they are mere witnesses. ☺

------- oooOooo ------

11 - Becoming an X-Rated Referee

The ageing process for referees accelerates as you reach the age of 50, as the editor has discovered.

I suppose I really began to think about it when I went to buy a new pair of football boots just before the start of the season. A young lady assistant came over to me as I looked on in bewilderment at the vast range of sports footwear facing me trying to work out what I wanted. "Can I help you?" she said. "Moulded sole football boots, size ten" I replied. "Who are they for?" "For me." It was her look of incredulous disbelief that first sent the pangs of ageing down my back and her reactive response "For You?" that reminded me, I'm fifty this year.

Fifty being a significant milestone in the life of a referee as you suddenly, it is alleged, have peaked and can progress no more. The 'X' that is added to your grade at that time is to stay with you the rest of your refereeing career like some brand across your forehead for all to observe and interpret as they see fit..

Now that I'm deemed to have reached the pinnacle of my refereeing career I reflect on life to date. I'm just entering my fourth season and already I've peaked! Each season I've been a different grade. From 3 to 2, to 1 last season and now a 1x. I feel that I've always been in a state of transition, I've never really been the fully finished product. Now the F.A. have decided that I am.

So what does it mean? Well in practice it means whatever grade you have now reached you will go no further. It doesn't mean that you are not to get prestigious appointments in the future.

What does it stand for? EXcellent?, eXtraordinary?, eXemplary? eXtinguished? or does it mean ex as in former? You tell me. Maybe it just means that I am a senior official now, whatever that means.

So what does it do to you as a referee. It's not helpful in that it tells everyone your age and signifies in the eyes of football that you no longer capable of progressing. Psychologically it forces a rethink on what you are doing. Should I be cutting back on my two games a weekend routine? Should I change my style of refereeing and not rely on fitness so much? Do I look for easier games?

I soon dismiss the idea of reducing my number of weekend games, football is addictive. Have you ever stood around in Marks & Spencers whilst the other half tries on some new outfit? Stand where you can see the towel displays. Watch how many women pass the display without feeling the thickness of the towels - None. It's in their make-up, it's a natural reaction, they can't go past without a quick feel. I'm the same about football, weekends mean football and as long as I'm able I suspect I will be available both on Saturdays and Sundays.

But wait, I get hold of a copy of the Huddersfield F.A. handbook finally and a quick check reveals that I'm still a Grade 1 - no 'x'. My birthday is not until December so I don't qualify until next season. I'm a bit disappointed now after coming to terms with my new status but I'm not worried about the addition when it comes next time around now that I've decided that 'X' stands for EXCEPTIONAL. ☺

------- oooOooo ------

12 - The Cardboard Cut-Out Ref

Do you really need a ref or would a cardboard cut-out suffice?

Many local Junior Soccer Leagues, both Saturday and Sunday, are desperately short of match officials and one has come up with a new and novel solution. You may well have noticed that in some Shopping Malls (you are allowed to go in them out of season) and on some motorways, life-size cardboard figures in the shape of policemen are being strategically placed to deter shoplifters and speeding motorists. Believe or not, it seems that results have proved that these figures are actually working well in preventing the would-be law breakers and crime is decreasing in the areas where they are used.

Not to be outdone, a local Referees' Secretary now issues similar cardboard figures of referees to teams when he cannot provide a real life official and results have been monitored which provide the following statistics:-

Where the cardboard ref is used (i.e. placed on the centre spot throughout the game)

> 50% of teams felt that the cardboard ref was worse than a real one;

> 25% of the teams felt that the cardboard ref was equally as good (or bad) as a real one;

> 25% of the teams felt that the cardboard ref was BETTER than a real one and insisted on using him for the rest of the season.

One club praised the cardboard ref for his mobility, they said that their usual refs never move at all throughout the game and that, at least, the cardboard ref fell over from time to time and even blew away without payment of fee at the end of the match. Is this the shape of things to come?

13 - Everybody has a Ref Story to Tell

No matter what level you play at everyone has their favourite referee story they like to relate over a pint, or over the phone or over often. Here are two of them.

The first comes from Paul Fletcher, once Chief Executive of Bolton Wanderers and the former England Under-21 international.

I was playing for Burnley when we were a top division club and due to play at Anfield on the coming Saturday. On the Friday the club made a new signing, 38 years old Mike Summerbee from Manchester City. Well known as bit of a character he was drafted straight into the team for the following days fixture.

Harry Potts was the team manager at that time, a strict disciplinarian, who had a rule that no player ever spoke to the referee never mind challenged a decision. Ignoring the rule brought the wrath of the mighty Harry down on you, something that no player of sound mind would invite.

In the Anfield visitor's changing room prior to kick-off with all the team stripped and ready for the fray, the match referee walked in. It was practice at this time for the match official to speak to both teams in an attempt to introduce harmony and understanding before kick-off.

The 6'2" official introduced himself and went on to outline how he would referee the game. Concluding by saying that he didn't anticipate any problems today - "You are professional footballers and I expect you to act like them. "I am a professional police inspector and will tolerate nothing less from you. "Any questions." As is custom in the Harry Pott's changing room nothing was said, that is until a voice from the corner - Mike Summerbee's voice - piped up "Yea, I've got a question - when you gonna catch Lord Lucan?" The room emptied double-quick time.

Into the game and Mr Summerbee continues to attract the referee's attention with his on field antics. Eventually this leads to a booking when the two come face to face again. "Name please," said the police inspector. "Well it's your lucky day Inspector cos it's Lord Lucan!" Yellow turned to red and the debutante heads for the tunnel and the undoubted warm reception from his new manager. ☺

The second Ref Story comes Total Football magazine's, Sales Executive, Steve Gardner, a keen local footballer.

The procedure in the League I play in is that the home club contacts the appointed referee four days in advance of the match to confirm the appointment. There is a well known 75 years-old referee who regularly turns out, as keen as the players and more mobile than some.

Our secretary rang his number to confirm the coming weekend's fixture, only to be answered by his wife. She informed him that her husband had just passed away and wouldn't be reffing this match or any more in the future.

Our secretary offered his condolences and thought little else of it until a few weeks later when this same referee turned up to officiate at an away game we played. We approached him and said how pleased we were to see him especially as his wife had told us he was dead. "She's always doing that if she gets to the phone before me," he said, "She doesn't like me refereeing nowadays and will do anything to stop me turning up. ☺

------- oooOooo ------

14 - Man Management Skills or a Cop Out?

Serious topic on how best to control 22 idiots hell-bent on Sunday morning violence.

I'm interested in this idea that, by using your man-management skills, referees can avoid problems on the pitch. Every time I listen to anyone talk about man-management skills it seems to be in the context of handling a difficult match or situation. And each time it appears to be used instead of cautioning or taking stronger action against players. I've come to the conclusion that in many instances it is used as an excuse for not taking the proper course of action that a deed deserves. In other words it's weak refereeing.

I listen to referees boasting that they haven't sent a player off all season and they give self credit to their man-management credentials. I wonder what the players think of those same referees, especially those at the sharp end of a bad tackle when the referee just uses his man-management skills to defuse the situation. Now I don't consider myself to be a 'booking-ref' (John Wilde will confirm this as he thinks I'm too soft, although I have had 18 yellows and 8 reds in my 41 games this season so far) but I cannot imagine going many games without issuing a card or two. I have tried a lenient approach. I've given players a 'last chance' instead of an easier booking and then regretted it when he continues to offend or when an opponent has noted my leniency and decided to extract his own justice.

Let me turn this argument around. Why shouldn't man-management skills mean cautioning more players? An early booking can set an example to all potential offenders, can reassure those that want to play football and reduce problems later in the game. Man-management isn't always about words, it's also about actions. Players understand actions better, as they are not so easily misinterpreted.

When I played football for one particular club the manager's approach was always to test out the mettle of the opponents and officials in the first ten minutes of every game. First corner-kick was always aimed underneath the crossbar so that two nominated players would put the keeper in the back of the net knowing that some of the more nervous type would then be watching for them, instead of the ball, at every high centre. First tackle on your opposite number had to be won, one way or another. You had to get the upper hand right from the off. Any free-kicks given away were always followed by loud apologies and a hand of friendship on the shoulder of the referee. Those refs that responded with a quiet word (or used man-management skills?) instead of the correct action, were not going to have an easy afternoon. If the referee let you get away with that then it was just opening the door for more of the same.

I have a stronger belief that your own personal skills are more important. That the way you treat players sets standards that you expect of them as well. For example I say 'Please' and 'Thankyou' a lot in a game. "Hurry the goalkick up please keeper." "Thankyou fella take the throw-in from there." I'm trying to show the respect that I would also like to receive. Lots of referees, at all levels, quote man-management as an important skill but I increasingly see it quoted as an excuse for not doing the job that we are there to do. Of course I may have got the message totally wrong so if anyone would like to explain to me what man-management skills are really about I would be delighted to hear from them.

------- oooOooo ------

15 - Shove A Whistle in It!

Classic quotations from and about referees over the years

My wife, who was in the stand, told me that at one stage the entire row in front of her stood up and gave me the V-sign. I asked her what she did and she said she didn't want them to know who she was, so she stood up and joined in.

Neil Midgley recalling his First Division debut

In all fairness the referee had a complete cerebral failure.

Rick Holden, Oldham 1995

Football wasn't meant to be run by two linesmen and air traffic control.

Tommy Docherty 1988

I'm having a crap game and nothing you will say will alter it.

Ian Barrett,

Norfolk referee to Crystal Palace manager Alan Smith 1993

For our game the referee was pleasant enough but a little erratic, a bit non-plussed by 22 fiercely competitive women.

Alyson Rudd, Leyton Orient Ladies striker

If we painted our footballs orange and threw one to a linesman, he'd probably try to peel it.

BASTARD IN BLACK

Jimmy Gabriel

The trouble with referees is that they just don't care who wins.

Tom Canterbury 1985

Referees belong to a sporting profession closely akin to that of a piano accompanist to great singers. Do the job perfectly and everyone applauds the singer. Strike just one wrong note and everyone, from the singer outwards, scowls and accuses you of ruining the performance.

Anon 1987

The referee was booking everyone. I thought he was doing his lottery numbers.

Ian Wright 1996

I know where he should have put his flag up and he'd have got plenty of help.

Ron Atkinson 1995

I have to hand it to Manchester United. They have the best players - and the best referees..

Sam Hamman, Wimbledon owner 1995

Integrity is what makes a good referee. It's not who is right but what is right.

Fred Burakat 1988

It's like a toaster that shirt pocket. Every time there's a tackle, up pops a yellow card.

Kevin Keegan 1994

I do like Selhurst Park. There's a Sainsburys right next to the ground so it's an ideal chance to get some of the weekend shopping out of the way.

David Elleray 1996

Referees are like politicians. They are never right.

Gerald Ford 1978

Thank God the referee and linesmen were out there together today, otherwise they could have spoiled three matches instead of one.

Tommy Docherty

Some referees are totally dedicated - to keeping fit, and parking as near to the dressing rooms as possible.

Anon

Making ex-players referees is a bit like putting a wife beater in charge of a marriage bureau.

Michael Parkinson

------- oooOooo ------

16 - The Early Laws of Association Football

Serious piece on the history of The Laws of the Game. Most people will skip this chapter just as they continue to ignore the present day set of Laws

Neil Simpson tells me that the earliest game resembling football was played in China around 400 B.C. and was called Tsu-Chu-Tsu (Kick with feet). Never one to doubt Neil's words, especially as he was probably lining that game with Don in the middle, however it is a fact that the laws of the game we use today are due to the young men at England's schools and universities in the mid-nineteenth century. There the codes of law necessary to allow two teams to compete on equal terms were first produced.

The public schools took the lead in writing down the rules of the game for others to follow. However each school had different ideas on the size of the pitch, the size and shape of the ball, how much handling was allowed and whether or not hacking was allowed.

In tracing the history of the game there are four sets of laws in particular that have made a significant contribution to today's game. They are Cambridge (1848). Sheffield (1857), Uppingham (1862) and the fledgling Football Association in 1863.

Remember that one set of rules did not supersede another, it was up to the schools or clubs to decide which set to adopt. Just imagine what chaos that would bring today, with the teams debating which set to use before the kick-off. In days gone by the clubs must have been much friendlier to have reached agreement prior to every game. Maybe they were just pleased that someone had attempted to bring some order to, what surely must have been, a chaotic situation.

The first attempt to formalise the rules of the game which received any credibility at all came from Cambridge University in 1848 as detailed below. This set of rules includes what may be the first reference to the offside law (see law 9 below) and is about as clear on that topic as today's interpretation but at least confused us in a lot less number of words.

These rules make no mention of the time duration of play, nothing on free-kicks or penalties, pitch dimensions remain a mystery and team colours and boots fail to get a mention.

After each goal the teams would change ends (unless a previous arrangement be made to the contrary) and holding, pushing and tripping were outlawed which wasn't the case in some of the alternative sets of rules to follow this early offering.

If you were to be transported back to the 1840's you could be forgiven for assuming that the group of young men playing with a large muddy object in open fields were engaged in a game of rugby rather than football, or maybe just a general brawl. If a player caught the ball he could run with it until tripped or hacked to the ground. Hacking was a sharp kick to the shins and perfectly legal in those days. Some of the players today still think it is.

If the ball was on the ground both sets of players would form a scrum around the ball and attempt to move forwards. Frequent rough play was accepted and you can imagine that tempers were short in the general melee that resulted. It is recorded that the players of the day were described as "a harmless set of lunatics who amused themselves by kicking one another's shins but did no great harm to the public at large".

The next of our four sets of rules it could be viewed as a step backwards for good sporting behaviour with charging and pushing amongst the listed fair play tactics. However hacking and tripping were specifically mentioned as not allowed much to the disgust of some of the more aggressive members of the clubs at that time.

This set of rules is believed to be the first established by a club as opposed to a school or university. The Sheffield rules of 1857, detailed below, were based on the Cambridge version. Pushing with the hands was allowed, but not tripping or hacking. Running with the ball in the hands (as practised at Rugby school) was not allowed. However the ball could be caught, provided it had not touched the ground; a free-kick then followed (similar to the "mark" in today's rugby football). The ball could also be pushed on with the hand.

There was no limit on team size and whatever shape of ball that happened to be handy was used. These rules do include the first reference to kit with every player charged with obtaining a red and a dark blue flannel cap, one colour to be worn by each team. There were no off-side rules, so players known as "kick-throughs" were positioned permanently in the opponents' half. Today they would be called goal poachers or lazy sods. And then finally there was no such thing as a referee, as the two captains would settle any dispute that may arise. Oh happy days - dream on.

CAMBRIDGE RULES 1848

1. This club shall be called the University Foot Ball Club.
2. At the commencement of play, the ball shall be kicked off from the middle of the ground; after every goal there shall be a kick-off in the same way or manner.
3. After a goal, the losing side shall kick-off; the sides change goals unless a previous arrangement be made to the contrary.
4. The ball is out when it has passed the line of the flag-post on either side of the ground, in which case it shall be thrown in straight.
5. The ball is "behind" when it has passed the goal on either side of it.
6. When the ball is behind, it shall be brought forward at the place where it left the ground not more than ten paces and kicked off.
7. Goal is when the ball is kicked through the flag-posts and under the string.
8. When a player catches the ball directly from the foot, he may kick it as he can without running with it. In no other case may the ball be touched with the hands, except to stop it.

9   If the ball has passed a player and has come from the direction of his own goal, he may not touch it till the other side have kicked it, unless there are more than three of the other side before him. No player is allowed to loiter between the ball and the adversaries goal.
10 In no case is holding a player, pushing with the hands or tripping up allowed. Any player may prevent another from getting to the ball by any means consistent with this rule.
11 Every match shall be decided by a majority of goals.

SHEFFIELD RULES 1857

1. The kick from the middle must be a place kick.
2. Kick out must not be more than 26 yards out of goal.
3. Fair catch is a catch from any player provided the ball has not touched the ground or has not been thrown from touch and is entitled to a free kick.
4. Charging is fair in case of a place kick (with the exception of a kick-off as soon as a player offers to kick) but he may always draw back unless he has touched the ball with his foot.
5. Pushing with the hands is allowed but no hacking or tripping up is fair under any circumstances whatever.
6. No player may be held or pulled over.
7. It is not unlawful to take the ball off the ground (except in touch) with any purpose whatever.
8. The ball may be pushed or hit with the hand, but holding the ball except in the case of a free kick is altogether disallowed.
9. A goal must be kicked but not from touch nor by a free kick from a catch.
10. A ball in touch is dead, consequently the side that touches it down must bring it to the edge of the touch and throw it straight out from touch.
11. Each player must provide himself with a red and a dark blue flannel cap, one colour to be worn by each side.

------- oooOooo ------

17 - Life Without Referees

Referees were mentioned for the first time in 1880, 32 years after the first set of rules were drawn up. Here's why.

Although the game started many years before any rules were formed it was still 32 years after the first set of rules provided by Cambridge University in 1848 that referees really appeared on the scene.

In the beginning the players didn't need a referee. They were gentlemen and any dispute could be settled by the two captains.

Of course this idyllic state of affairs couldn't last, especially when competitive soccer in the form of the Football Association's Cup came along in 1872. By this time it had become the practice for each team to appoint an umpire. These two gentlemen then ran about the pitch, keeping an eye on matters. They had no right to interfere with the game but could be 'appealed to' by the players just as in the game of cricket today.

They were given the power to award a free-kick for handball in 1873 and for other offences in 1874. Also in this year, umpires could send a player off for 'persistent infringement of the rules'.

Of course it is not surprising that occasionally the two umpires could not agree on a decision and so the need arose for a neutral observer, the "referee". The first mention of the referee occurs in 1880. He was appointed by mutual agreement of the two clubs. He was required to 'keep a record of the game' and act as timekeeper. He had the power to caution players who were guilty of ungentlemanly conduct, without consulting the umpires (though any such caution was made with the umpires present). If a player continued to transgress, or was guilty of violent conduct, the referee could send him off and report him, even if the player then proffered an apology.

The referee was given greater powers in 1889/90 when he was allowed to award a free-kick for foul play without waiting for an appeal. It was only at this point that he needed a whistle. The well known story that the referee's whistle was first used at a Nottingham Forest v Sheffield Norfolk game in 1878 must be viewed with scepticism. Forest didn't play Norfolk in that season and the referee had no need for a whistle anyway.

Not until the 1891/92 season was he finally given the powers he has today, and allowed onto the field of play. It was at this stage that the two umpires assumed the role of linesmen and we have the set-up as it is today.

------- oooOooo ------

18 - Things You No Longer See At Football Grounds
A nostalgic look back at football when I was a lad.

Rattles: Hand-operated wooden device which produced clacking sound intended to fire up 'the lads' or strike fear into hearts of the enemy. Could be painted in club colours. Fell into disuse purportedly because of possible use as weapon. Actually fell into disuse because they were crap.

Rosettes: Ludicrous twinning of satin and cardboard which made wearer, if Blackpool supporter, resemble canvasser for Liberal Party.

Milk Crates: Dads obtained them under mysterious circumstances, then carried them miles to grounds in semi-Arctic conditions just so junior's view of game would not be obscured by heads of folk in front. Real men in them days..., today's seated nippers don't know they're born..., etc
.
Silk Scarves: One around each wrist was the perfect accessory to match your tank top, 24-inch flared cords and Alan Biley-effect feather-cut mullet.

Invalid Cars': Main reason why supporters used to pack ground a full half-hour before appearance of teams was not, as generally imagined, to secure best standing position, but rather to witness 2.45pm convoy of blue three-wheelers which would circle cinder track on outside of pitch before settling for ringside view of proceedings. Where did they all go?

Thermos Flasks: By law, could contain either Bovril or Heinz Tomato Soup (night matches only). Usually tartan.

Oversized Badges: Today's kids can pledge allegiance to Manchester United with aid of stylish New York Yankees-style baseball cap. Forebearers, however, were forced to deal with lapels groaning under weight of virtually life-size visage of Alan Brazil.

Socks Referred to In Programme As 'Stockings': Children across country wept when snigger-inducing Olde Worlde Speake disappeared in late 1970s. (reportedly still uttered on occasion by 5 Live's more senior commentators).

The Orange Ball: In Football League, used only on snowiest of days. In your Subbuteo set, used in every match.

Bobble Hats: Once bestrode football headgear market like a woollen colossus. In devil's bargain, however, openly coveting one led to awful home-knit possibilities...

Pre-Miniaturisation Radios Perched On One Shoulder: Long years of Hunchbackery which inevitably followed were all presumably worth it for thrill of being able to answer in affirmative when asked, "Know the Liverpool score, mate?"

Toilet Rolls Thrown Onto Pitch: Advent of fluffy soft toilet paper - a rapid advance in comfort, but lacking unfurling qualities of Izal - killed craze off.

Alphabet 'Scoreboard': Huge board bearing capital letters A-J was filled in at half-time by small boys bearing huge plastic numbers. Hence you knew that match A stood at 2-1, match B 1-0, etc. What you didn't know was what match A actually was. Unless you bought a programme.

Fans Changing Ends Between Halves: In Good Old Days, ref's half-time whistle was cue for gates opening to allow en-masse traipse around perimeter of ground, ostensibly so fans could stand behind goal being attacked by their own team for full 90 minutes. Fact that doing so meant opposing fans had to pass each other inevitably led to scenes reminiscent of final reel of Zulu.

Two-Sided Ski Hats With Name Of Favourite English Club On One Side And Name Of One Of The Glasgow Giants On The Other: Slight possibility that religious bigotry may have been involved here...

Huge Oval Tracks Around Larger Grounds: Three per cent of population interested in speedway/greyhound racing thought they were great. Other 97 per cent of us cursed them on a bi-weekly basis as long-awaited annual look at Georgie Best was spoiled by fact that he was visible only through high-powered binoculars.

High-Powered Binoculars: See above.

Piles Of Shoe Laces At Turnstiles: For Chelsea fans only. In hooligan heyday of 1970s, skinheads would have to remove laces from Doc Martens prior to entry into 'Bridge', presumably so mass suicides could not occur.

Numbered Sock Flaps: reckoned to be part of football fashion in Year 2000 when sported by Leeds United in 1970s. In fact, were as much a part of future of football as United striker Ray Hankin.

Shorts Referred To In Programme As 'Knickers': Never mind the socks/stockings interface mentioned yesterday, this was even better...

------- oooOooo ------

19 - Refereeing Acronyms

Every industry, profession and culture seems to live by acronyms – initials of regular terminology – the football referee is no different although some of these may be new to you.

Interfering Outside Agents - KGB, CIA or FBI?

I remember when I first came across this refereeing term 'Interference from an outside agent' it conjured up a picture of cigarette smoking men in long mac's, trilbys and dark glasses - and in that description, any passing resemblance to assessors is totally unintentional, I promise! Whilst I distance myself from such underworld happenings a number of things have happened to me and colleagues which come under that 'interference' heading.

KGB. (Kid Grabs Ball)

In one match a toddler ran into the penalty area and picked up the ball at his father's feet. Luckily his father was defending at the time with no-one - or so he thought - around him. We retrieved the ball from a disgruntled 2 year old and I dropped the ball at the feet of a rather embarrassed dad - no other players came near.

CIA (Collie in Attack)

To be honest it was much larger than a Collie (more like an Alsation) and much harder to catch than a toddler. It didn't actually attack anyone either, but its defence strategy was impressive and its avoidance of capture raised a few smiles from spectators. At the time I lost track of exactly where the ball was when the dog first 'interfered' and the players weren't sure either. I dropped the ball on the halfway line and one team volunteered to kick it back to the opposing goal-keeper (not too hard!) - so who says sportsmanship is dead - and it wasn't even their dog!

FBI (Fallen Branch Interferes)

Yes, it really was a branch which fell off a tree when the ball hit it - not one I'd over-looked during the pitch inspection. Luckily it didn't hit anyone and it wasn't a very special branch either (O.K. O.K. awful joke, I know). Over-hanging trees are not so unusual and many pitches have trees close to them with high branches which don't get cut back as often as lower ones.

Unfortunately, or fortunately, chain-saws aren't a part of the referees normal equipment (a possible suggestion at the last meeting!) and I wouldn't recommend tree surgery just before a game.

If you do have this problem the chances of getting anything done before the game are slim but you should suggest to the home team or the groundsman that something is done about over-hanging branches as soon as possible. You should also mention it on your match result card or in a separate letter to the League concerned to make them aware.

During the game if the ball makes any contact with part of the tree within the field of play you drop the ball at the closest point below where the contact was made.

WI (Whistle Interference)

No, I don't mean an over-enthusiastic referee but a whistle heard on another pitch which causes the players to hesitate or stop and 'interferes' with the course of the game. Many referees carry a whistle with a different tone and change whistles if they think this can be of help (sometimes players just stop at any whistle and as we know, some don't stop at any whistle!).

On occasions I've shouted "Not my whistle lads - carry on" and the game has continued without a problem. I will only stop if I feel an advantage or disadvantage has occurred.

Occasionally we may find we have a 'phantom whistler amongst the spectators, or even the players. Obviously this can undermine your authority as well as affect the game immediately and if it happens more than once you may need to talk to the captains or managers to find the culprit It is within your powers to act against a player who is guilty of 'Unsporting behaviour' or warn a club they could be reported if their spectators misbehave.

CBE (Cardboard Box - Empty!)

On a windy day a cardboard box blew across the goal-keeper as a shot came in on goal. Luckily no goal was scored and the ball went for a goal-kick The 'keeper asked me what I would have done if the ball had gone in and I went up in his estimation when I said it wouldn't have been a goal but a drop ball from where I'd judged the 'interference' or distraction had first occurred (it was outside the goal area).

BHS. (Ball Hits Seagull)

Or any other bird or flying object for that matter i.e. ball from another pitch. Often balls from other pitches will enter your pitch and will get kicked away or collected. As long as they don't interfere, you don't need to stop the game.

C&A (Cars and Ambulances)

There have been incidents of cars being driven across pitches during games - on one occasion at the referee! I would recommend match abandonment in this case rather than a drop ball!

Only recently I witnessed a player injured and the need for an ambulance to be called. His team-mates decided he was moveable and carried him across the goal-line so the game could be resumed. Unfortunately the ambulance arrived and parked on the pitch whilst the game continued. I certainly would never question a referees eye-sight but this was a normal sized ambulance - large and white - and the referee did look around. The game continued and luckily the players didn't decide to play any one, twos off the side of the ambulance and it drove away without any direct interfering. Not something I'd recommend really as an attacking team might get more disgruntled than players in the middle of the park when you stop the game.

I'm sure that many other stories could be told about this subject and I'm sure you've had interference at times. Let me re-phrase that............ Perhaps you've been the referee who has witnessed little Billy's irate mother cuff an opponent around the ear for depriving her son of the ball or had a stray Frisbee, golf, cricket or tennis ball knock someone out from a nearby park, course, pitch or court.

What did you do? STOP PLAY and restart by DROPPING THE BALL 'at the place where it was located when play was stopped' unless it was in the goal area, in which case I hope you brought it out to the goal area line parallel to the goal line before dropping it.

------- oooOooo ------

20 - The Flexible Rules of Playground Football

You needed a special set of unwritten rules to survive school playtime.

DURATION

Matches shall be played over three unequal periods: two playtimes and a lunchtime.

Each of these periods shall begin shortly after the ringing of a bell, and although a bell is also rung towards the end of these periods, play may continue for up to ten minutes afterwards, depending on the nihilism or "bottle" of the participants with regard to corporal punishment met out to latecomers back to the classroom.
In practice there is a sliding scale of nihilism, from those who hasten to stand in line as soon as the bell rings, known as "poofs", through those who will hang on until the time they estimate it takes the teachers to down the last of their gins and journey from the staffroom, known as "chancers", and finally to those who will hang on until a teacher actually has to physically retrieve them, known as "bampots".

This sliding scale is intended to radically alter the logistics of a match in progress, often having dramatic effects on the scoreline as the number of remaining participants drops. It is important, therefore, in picking the sides, to achieve a fair balance of poofs, chancers and bampots in order that the scoreline achieved over a sustained period of play - a lunchtime, for instance - is not totally nullified by a five-minute post-bell onslaught of five bampots against one.

The scoreline to be carried over from the previous period of the match is in the trust of the last bampots to leave the field of play, and may be the matter of some debate. This must be resolved in one of the approved manners (see Adjudication).

PARAMETERS

The object is to force the ball between two large, unkempt piles of jackets, in lieu of goalposts. These piles may grow or shrink throughout the match, depending on the number of participants and the prevailing weather. As the number of players increases, so shall the piles. Each jacket added to the pile by a new addition to a side should be placed on the inside, nearest the goalkeeper, thus reducing the target area. It is also important that the sleeve of one of the jackets should jut out across the goalmouth, as it will often be claimed that the ball went "over the post" and it can henceforth be asserted that the outstretched sleeve denotes the innermost part of the pile and thus the inside of the post. The on-going reduction of the size of the goal is the responsibility of any respectable defence and should be undertaken conscientiously with resourcefulness and imagination

In the absence of a crossbar, the upper limit of the target area is observed as being slightly above head height, although when the height at which a ball passed between the jackets is in dispute, judgement shall lie with an arbitrary adjudicator from one of the sides. He is known as the "best fighter"; his decision is final and may be enforced with physical violence if anyone wants to stretch a point.

There are no pitch markings. Instead, physical objects denote the boundaries, ranging from the most common - walls and buildings - to roads or burns. Corners and throw-ins are redundant where bylines or touchlines are denoted by a two-storey building or a six-foot granite wall. Instead, a scrum should be instigated to decide possession. This should begin with the ball trapped between the brickwork and two opposing players, and should escalate to include as many team members as can get there before the now egg-shaped ball finally emerges, drunkenly and often with a dismembered foot and shin attached. At this point, goalkeepers should look out for the player who takes possession of the escaped ball and begins bearing down on goal, as most of those involved in the scrum will be unaware that the ball is no longer amidst their feet. The goalkeeper should also try not to be distracted by the inevitable fighting that has by this point broken out.

In games on large open spaces, the length of the pitch is obviously denoted by the jacket piles, but the width is a variable. In the absence of roads, water hazards or "a big dug"(dog), the width is determined by how far out the attacking winger has to meander before the pursuing defender gets fed up and lets him head back towards where the rest of the players are waiting, often as far as quarter of a mile away. It is often observed that the playing area is "no' a full-size pitch". This can be invoked verbally to justify placing a wall of players eighteen inches from the ball at direct free kicks It is the formal response to "yards", which the kick-taker will incant meaninglessly as he places the ball.

THE BALL

There is a variety of types of ball approved for Primary School Football. I shall describe three notable examples.

1. The plastic balloon. An extremely lightweight model, used primarily in the early part of the season and seldom after that due to having burst. Identifiable by blue pentagonal panelling and the names of that year's Premier League sides printed all over it. Advantages: low sting factor, low burst-nose probability, cheap, discourages a long-ball game. Disadvantages: over-susceptible to influence of the wind, difficult to control, almost magnetically drawn to flat school roofs whence never to return.

2. The rough-finish Mitre. Half football, half Portuguese Man o' War. On the verge of a ban in the European Court of Human Rights, this model is not for sale to children. Used exclusively by teachers during gym classes as a kind of aversion therapy. Made from highly durable fibre-glass, stuffed with neutron star and coated with dead jellyfish. Advantages: looks quite grown up, makes for high-scoring matches (keepers won't even attempt to catch it). Disadvantages: scars or maims anything it touches.

3. The "Tubey". Genuine leather ball, identifiable by brown all-over colouring. Was once black and white, before ravages of games on concrete, but owners can never remember when. Adored by everybody, especially keepers. Advantages: feels good, easily controlled, makes a satisfying "whump" noise when you kick it. Disadvantages: turns into medicine ball when wet, smells like a dead dog.

OFFSIDE

There is no offside, for two reasons: one, "it's no' a full-size pitch", and two, none of the players actually know what offside is. The lack of an offside rule gives rise to a unique sub-division of strikers. These players hang around the opposing goalmouth while play carries on at the other end, awaiting a long pass forward out of defence which they can help past the keeper before running the entire length of the pitch with their arms in the air to greet utterly imaginary adulation. These are known variously as "poachers", "gloryhunters" and "fly wee bastarts". These players display a remarkable degree of self-security, seemingly happy in their own appraisals of their achievements, and caring little for their team-mates' failure to appreciate the contribution they have made. They know that it can be for nothing other than their enviable goal tallies that they are so bitterly despised.

ADJUDICATION

The absence of a referee means that disputes must be resolved between the opposing teams rather than decided by an arbiter. There are two accepted ways of doing this.

1. Compromise. An arrangement is devised that is found acceptable by both sides. Sway is usually given to an action that is in accordance with the spirit of competition, ensuring that the game does not turn into "a pure skoosh". For example, in the event of a dispute as to whether the ball in fact crossed the line, or whether the ball has gone inside or "over" the post, the attacking side may offer the ultimatum: "Penalty or

goal." It is not recorded whether any side has ever opted for the latter. It is on occasions that such arrangements or ultimata do not prove acceptable to both sides that the second adjudicatory method comes into play.

2. Fighting. Those up on their ancient Hellenic politics will understand that the concept we know as "justice" rests in these circumstances with the hand of the strong. What the winner says, goes, and what the winner says is just, for who shall dispute him? It is by such noble philosophical principles that the supreme adjudicator, or Best Fighter, is effectively elected.

TEAM SELECTION

To ensure a fair and balanced contest, teams are selected democratically in a turns-about picking process, with either side beginning as a one-man selection committee and growing from there. The initial selectors are usually the recognised two Best Players of the assembled group. Their first selections will be the two recognised Best Fighters, to ensure a fair balance in the adjudication process, and to ensure that they don't have their own performances impaired throughout the match by profusely bleeding noses. They will then proceed to pick team-mates in a roughly meritocratic order, selecting on grounds of skill and tactical awareness, but not forgetting that while there is a sliding scale of players' ability, there is also a sliding scale of players' brutality and propensities towards motiveless violence. A selecting captain might baffle a talented striker by picking the less nimble Big Jazza ahead of him, and may explain, perhaps in the words of Linden B Johnson upon his retention of J Edgar Hoover as the head of the FBI, that he'd "rather have him inside the tent pissing out, than outside the tent pissing in". Special consideration is also given during the selection process to the owner of the ball. It is tacitly acknowledged to be "his gemme", and he must be shown a degree of politeness for fear that he takes the huff at being picked late and withdraws his favours.

Another aspect of team selection that may confuse those only familiar with the game at senior level will be the choice of goalkeepers, who will inevitably be the last players to be picked. Unlike in the senior game, where the goalkeeper is often the tallest member of his team, in the playground, the goalkeeper is usually the smallest. Senior aficionados must appreciate that playground selectors have a different agenda and are looking for altogether different properties in a goalkeeper. These can be listed briefly as: compliance, poor fighting ability, meekness, fear and anything else that makes it easier for their team-mates to banish the wee bugger between the sticks while they go off in search of personal glory up the other end.

TACTICS

Playground football tactics are best explained in terms of team formation. Whereas senior sides tend to choose - according to circumstance - from among a number of standard options (eg 4-4-2, 4-3-3, 5-3-2), the playground side is usually more rigid in sticking to the all-purpose 1-1-17 formation. This formation is a sturdy basis for the unique style of play, ball-flow and territorial give-and-take that makes the playground game such a renowned and strategically engrossing spectacle. Just as the 5-3-2 formation is sometimes referred to in practice as "Cattenaccio", the 1-1-17 formation gives rise to a style of play that is best described as "Nomadic". All but perhaps four of the participants (see also Offside) migrate en masse from one area of the pitch to another, following the ball, and it is tactically vital that every last one of them remains within a ten-yard radius of it at all times.

Much stoppage time in the senior game is down to injured players requiring treatment on the field of play. The playground game flows freer having adopted the refereeing philosophy of "no Post-Mortem, no free-kick", and play will continue around and even on top of a participant who has fallen in the course of his endeavours. However, the playground game is nonetheless subject to other interruptions, and some examples are listed below.

Ball on school roof or over school wall. The retrieval time itself is negligible in these cases. The stoppage is most prolonged by the argument to decide which player must risk life, limb or four of the belt to scale the drainpipe or negotiate the barbed wire in order to return the ball to play. Disputes usually arise between the player who actually struck the ball and any others he claims it may have struck before disappearing into forbidden territory. In the case of the Best Fighter having been adjudged responsible for such an incident, a volunteer is often required to go in his stead or the game may be abandoned, as the Best Fighter is entitled to observe that A: "Ye canny make me"; or B: "It's no' ma baw anyway".

Stray dog on pitch. An interruption of unpredictable duration. The dog does not have to make off with the ball, it merely has to run around barking loudly, snarling and occasionally drooling or foaming at the mouth. This will ensure a dramatic reduction in the number of playing staff as 27 of them simultaneously volunteer to go indoors and inform the teacher of the threat. The length of the interruption can sometimes be gauged by the breed of dog. A deranged Irish Setter could take ten minutes to tire itself of running in circles, for instance, while a Jack Russell may take up to fifteen minutes to corner and force out through the gates. An Alsatian means instant abandonment.

STOPPAGES

Bigger boys steal ball. A highly irritating interruption, the length of which is determined by the players' experience in dealing with this sort of thing. The intruders will seldom actually steal the ball, but will improvise their own kickabout amongst themselves, occasionally inviting the younger players to attempt to tackle them. Standing around looking bored and unimpressed usually results in a quick restart. Shows of frustration and engaging in attempts to win back the ball can prolong the stoppage indefinitely. Informing the intruders that one of the players' older brother is "Mad Chic Murphy" or some other noted local pugilist can also ensure minimum delay.

Menopausal old bag confiscates ball. More of a threat in the street or local green kickabout than within the school walls. Sad, blue-rinsed, ill-tempered, Tory-voting cat-owner transfers her anger about the array of failures that has been her life to nine-year-olds who have committed the heinous crime of letting their ball cross her privet Line of Death. Interruption (loss of ball) is predicted to last "until you learn how to play with it properly", but instruction on how to achieve this without actually having the bloody thing is not usually forwarded. Tact is required in these circumstances, even when the return of the ball seems highly unlikely, as further irritation of woman may result in the more serious stoppage:
Menopausal old bag calls police.

CELEBRATION

Goal-scorers are entitled to a maximum run of thirty yards with their hands in the air, making crowd noises and saluting imaginary packed terraces. Congratulation by team-mates is in the measure appropriate to the importance of the goal in view of the current scoreline (for instance, making it 34-12 does not entitle the player to drop to his knees and make the sign of the cross), and the extent of the scorer's contribution. A fabulous solo dismantling of the defence or 25-yard* rocket shot will elicit applause and back-pats from the entire team and the more magnanimous of the opponents. However, a tap-in in the midst of a chaotic scramble will be heralded with the epithet "poachin' wee bastart" from the opposing defence amidst mild acknowledgment from team-mates. Applying an unnecessary final touch when a ball is already rolling into the goal will elicit a burst nose from the original striker. Kneeling down to head the ball over the line when defence and keeper are already beaten will elicit a thoroughly deserved kicking. As a footnote, however, it should be stressed that any goal scored by the Best Fighter will be met with universal acclaim, even if it falls into any of the latter three categories.

*Actually eight yards, but calculated as relative distance because "it's no' a full-size pitch".

PENALTIES

At senior level, each side often has one appointed penalty-taker, who will defer to a team-mate in special circumstances, such as his requiring one more for a hat-trick. The playground side has two appointed penalty-takers: the Best Player and the Best Fighter. The arrangement is simple: the Best Player takes the penalties when his side is a retrievable margin behind, and the Best Fighter at all other times. If the side is comfortably in front, the ball-owner may be invited to take a penalty.

Goalkeepers are often the subject of temporary substitutions at penalties, forced to give up their position to the Best Player or Best Fighter, who recognise the kudos attached to the heroic act of saving one of these kicks, and are buggered if Wee Titch is going to steal any of it.

CLOSE SEASON

This is known also as the Summer Holidays, which the players usually spend dabbling briefly in other sports: tennis for a fortnight while Wimbledon is on the telly; pitch-and-putt for four days during the Open; and cricket for about an hour and a half until they discover that it really is as boring to play as it is to watch.

------- oooOooo ------

21 - Ten Things We Really Love To See At A Football Match

No-one likes to see that... oh yes they do... Ten things we love to see at a football match.

A hatful of goals, loads of chances and some moments of brilliant individual skill in a hard-fought but gentlemanly contest. Surely the recipe for the ideal football match? Absolutely not. What you really want is the chance to see players, referees, supporters and managers doing bizarre or embarrassing things. Here's a few suggestions of the vital ingredients for a really enjoyable match...

1) The Referee Makes A Fool Of Himself

Comes in many guises. Sending off the wrong player and having to chase after him, being struck amidships by a powerful drive and producing the wrong coloured card are all enjoyable, of course. The favourite, though, is the referee pratfall, ideally after treading on the ball, as recently demonstrated to stunning effect by Stephen Lodge.

2) The Mascots Have A Right Old Dust-Up

Club spokespersons are forever telling us: "The kids love Harry The Hammer/Roary The Tiger/ Kevin The Pike" etc. The only people who really take any interest in the creatures, of course, are the thousands of adults. They're hoping beyond hope that it'll all go off between the two "resting" actors who have been in the pub all day trying to drown out the humiliation before getting into their ridiculous furry suits.

3) The Manager Is Sent From The Dug Out

A series of iffy decisions have sent the gaffer into an apoplectic fury. A calm but steely response is clearly essential. Up steps the fourth official, a whey-faced accountant from Edgerton. Obviously terrified, he attempts to usher the snarling manager away from the scene, nearly losing his teeth in the process.

4) The Missed Penalty

Obvious, but nonetheless eternally amusing. Your pre-Jurassic centre half, a player with all the mobility and grace of a skip, has just scythed down the opposition's brilliant, quicksilver young striker in the box. The inevitable penalty is given, and the RADA-trained forward suddenly makes a miraculous recovery from his life-threatening injuries. He steps up to take it himself, utterly convinced that he will score. He misses. Hilariously. The shot dribbles pathetically wide of the post and thousands of grown men do their bit for the Nescafé magic beans campaign.

5) The Attempt To Get An Opponent Booked

A comparatively new phenomenon, this, and one much tut-tutted over by ex-pros and the media. But let's be honest... Is there any funnier sight in football than an irate, ideally very short, player chasing the referee around the pitch frantically wagging an imaginary card? We would suggest not.

6) The Own Goal

Ideally, this should be the result of a sickening, trigonometry-defying deflection of 30 yards or more that loops over the helpless keeper. However, many make the case for the over hit back-pass or the flying defensive header that thunders into the roof of the net. And it's so much more satisfying than one of your own players scoring.

7) The Female Streaker

Modern TV may give you the benefit of super slo-mo, hundreds of different camera angles and the excitement of an expert doodling on the screen with a light, felt-tip pen, but if you're going to see that pair of large, misshapen breasts exposed to the biting elements and hordes of pie-munching blokes singing obscene songs in sheer, unadulterated delight, then nowadays you'll have to pay at the turnstile like your granddad did.

8) The Huge On-Pitch Barney

Pundits and journalists invariably take a censorious stance over these, calling immediately for the offending players to be banned for several years, or deported, or possibly just exterminated. But surely nothing livens up a dull 0-0 more than a good old-fashioned ruck? Furthermore, footballers seem totally unable to fight properly, forever slapping or pushing each other in a highly camp manner and rarely, if ever, hurting each other.

9) The Solo Four-Legged Pitch Invasion

Invariably amusing, but particularly so if the animal in question attempts to swallow/puncture/head the ball. Strong possibility of defecation as the creature becomes overwhelmed by the noise. Dogs are obviously the most common source here, but cats, foxes, badgers and stags have all graced British football grounds in their time.

10) The Tiny Children In Half-Time Shoot-Out They appear impossibly small on the pitch, in some instances the ball seeming to come up almost to their waist. The club has dug out the smallest kits they could possibly find, but the shorts are still dragging along the turf and the socks are pulled up to eye-level. One little lad dribbles towards the goal and the equally tiny keeper comes out to meet him, bringing him down in the process. "Off! Off! Off!" shout the crowd. A bit mean. A bit funny.

------- oooOooo ------

22 - World Cup 2014: The Alternative Team Squads

Its World Cup year again and the time for us to be entranced by the new names and stars that emerge from the competition. We are pleased to share with you this alternative list of squad players from some teams.

BRAZIL

In Brazil, where football is only marginally less popular than sex, an unusually high proportion of shoeless urchins make it in to the big time. Let's face it, if one minute you're living in a dustbin in a shanty town with twelve members of your family and the next you're sitting in your hilltop villa with hot and cold running toilets, you'd be motivated as well

Team:

Pinnochio

Libero

Vimto Memento Borneo Tango

Cheerio Subbuteo

Scenario Fellatio Portfolio

Subs:
Placebo, Porno, Polio ,Banjo, Brasso, Stereo(L), Stereo (R), Hydrochlorofluoro (GK) Aristotle

ITALY

It's often said that the Italians are the footballing aristocrats of Europe. Presumably that means that they're stupid, inbred and prone to behave like spoilt children when they don't get their own way. One has to doubt the sanity of any millionaire footballer who drives a Fiat. If it wasn't for the fact that Mr Fiat openly owned the club the player plays for, or the Mafia connections behind it dictating what toothpaste you use through to what car you drive, then you just do as you're told

Team:

                              Baloni

            Potbelli   Beerbelli   Giveitsumwelli

       Wotsontelli   Toonsgotkenni   Onetoomani

               Legslikejelli   Havabenni

                Wobblijelli   Spendapenni

Subs: Buggermi, Cantthinkofani!!

BEST OF THE REST

Insufficient space to list all the squads but some of the rest have distinct advantages by coming from where they do. Like the French - because everyone thinks you're a great lover even when you're not; you don't have to read the sub-titles on late night films and you don't have to bother with toilets you just shit in the street. The Spanish who make the best paella while the rest of the world copy it and claim theirs as the best, and the licence to dress up stupid in tight clothes and risk your life in front of bulls and then bed the best looking women. We never had a chance really

GREECE

Team:

                    Chatanoogaciouciou

          Atishiou   Blessiou   Thankyiou

        Busqueue   Snookercu

      Pennyciou Twoapennyciou Fourapennyciou

           I'llgetciou Youandwhosarmi

Subs: U, NonU, ManU, Stuffyiou, Lee Kwan Yu

RUSSIA

<u>Team:</u>

                              Whodyanicabolicov

                Ticlycov   Chesticov   Nasticov

       Slalomsky   Downhillsky

          Risky   Swedishshev   Mastershev

                   Fuckov   Taykitov

SUBS: Rubitov, Whisky, Pastyshev, Najinsky, Desert Orchid

SWITZERLAND

<u>Team:</u>

                              Toomanigoalssen

      Tryandstopussen   Crapdefenssen   Haveagossen

         Firstsson   Seccondsson   Thirdsson

            Legshurtssen   Notroubleseeingussen

                Wherestheballssen   Getthebeerssen

<u>Subs:</u> Howmanygoalsisthatssen
        Finallygaveupcountinssen
        Hurryupandblowthewhistlessen
        Yourelatedtoalexfergusonssen

MEXICO

Team:

San Francisco

Costa Brava   Hopelez   Juan Andonly   Manuel Gearbox

Don Cryformeargentina   Bodegas   Luis Canon   Sombrero

Chihuahua   Jose Canyouseebythedawnsearlylight

Subs: Jesus Maria Don Key, Burrito, Speedy Gonzalez, Tequila, Caramba

CROATIA

Team:

Itch

Annoyingitch   Hardtoreachitch   Scratchtheitch

Hic(k)   Sic   Spic   Pric

Digaditch   Fallinaditch   Sewastitch

Subs: Mowapitch, Letsgetrich, Shagabitch

SCOTLAND

They wont be in Brazil but judging on past performances if they were, they would once again win the Best Supporters/Worst Team Award. Don't they make you sick? They come as no-hopers and fail to live up to their own low expectations but the fans engage everyone and pull all the decent looking local birds with their honest, sober, generous approach to life. The Scottish Supporters Club (Motto: If you can lay in a gutter without holding on you're not really drunk) got tickets for both their members so why couldn't the England Supporters Club? Thank goodness they aren't going to be there. We name their squad anyhow because it amuses us to do so.

Team:
                    Phil MacCracken

        Bill MaCreditcard   Willy O'Wontie
            Chuck MaLoad   Ben Dover

        Luke Atmadick   Fartoolong McStay
            Jack Mabody   Tam Furalastyin

        Afore Thechippyshuts   Whitsthe Hampden

Subs:
Roger Yerarse, Coisty (as always), Jim Jimeny
Alf Uckentakehislegsaway
Bruce Yerselvesforanotherclosemiss
Geeza Quickyhen(ex foreign-national)
Some Unknown Youngster

------- oooOooo ------

23 - Refereeing Horoscopes

The official forecast for officials for the coming week-end are officially as follows

Even some referees have futures and the stars hold the key, just as they do for normal people.

AQUARIUS

A lot of possibilities have opened up and will make you more indecisive than usual. Even when you make a choice it will be queried by many.

PISCES

Your winning personality endears you to others as you make people feel wanted. Enjoy the warm glow of being popular today. Lucky Colour: Yellow.

ARIES

An outburst would clear the air but could damage fragile relationships. You certainly don't want to make someone feel guilty if they are innocent.

TAURUS

Shoving your head in the sand and hoping the problem will go away is foolish, so take time to re-examine the evidence and then take action.

GEMINI

You are let down by a friend wearing black who you have become to rely upon. His attention seeking antics irritate and you should continue to ignore him.

CANCER

Helping others is a Cancerian trait but don't get caught up in other people's problems as you have quite a few of your own to solve today.

LEO

Although you are very caring, you also need to be cared for – and others don't always realise this. Today is one of those days. Lucky Colour: Red.

VIRGO

Try to steer clear of crowded places this weekend as this is a time when you prefer to be on your own with nobody to account to but yourself.

LIBRA

You try to maintain your neutrality but this weekend is a time to show your favouritism to those you like. A good time to be investing in life insurance.

SCORPIO

The best weekend of the year for making new friends and exchanging names with them. You are bound to see them again so cheer up and enjoy it.

SAGITTARIUS

You appear to have upset someone but you don't know how. Don't delve too deep, just ignore them and they'll come back if they want to.

CAPRICORN

Don't be intimidated by others who follow the popular opinion. Stick with your views and don't be afraid to stand up and be counted. Lucky number 9.

------- oooOooo ------

24 - Twenty Reasons Why Sex Is Better Than Football

1. No match fees

2. It takes less than ninety minutes

3. Studs are optional

4. You have fewer people watching you

5. It doesn't matter if it rains

6. There are no penalties

7. No wall in front of goal

8. Screaming is encouraged

9. You control the kick-off time

10. You won't have to pay the referee

11. Ball cleaning is not a chore

12. No goalie stopping your shots

13. There are no free-kicks

14. Less profanity

15. No one is wearing cycling shorts

16. A whistle doesn't go to tell you it's finished.

17. Your parents don't cheer when you score.

18. You don't have to wait to the weekend to play

19. Boring team-mates don't relate all the details about how they scored.

20. You can't be substituted.

------- oooOooo ------

25 - American Football is Dead

An open letter to the citizens of the United States of America.

Further to your abortive invasions of Vietnam, Iraq and Afghanistan and thus the inability to govern yourselves properly, we hereby give notice of the revocation of your independence, effective today. Her Sovereign Majesty Queen Elizabeth II will resume monarchial duties over all states, commonwealths and other territories. Except Utah, which she does not fancy.

Your new prime minister (The Rt. Hon. David Cameron MP for the 97.85% of you who have until now been unaware that there is a world outside your borders) will appoint a minister for America without the need for further elections. Congress and the Senate will be disbanded. A questionnaire will be circulated next year to determine whether any of you noticed.

To aid in the transition to a British Crown Dependency, the following rules are introduced with immediate effect:

1. You should look up "revocation" in the Oxford English Dictionary. Then look up "aluminium". Check the pronunciation guide. You will be amazed at just how wrongly you have been pronouncing it. Generally, you should raise your vocabulary to acceptable levels. Look up "vocabulary". Using the same twenty seven words interspersed with filler noises such as "like" and "you know" is an unacceptable and inefficient form of communication. Look up "interspersed".

2. There is no such thing as "US English". We will let Microsoft know on your behalf.

3. You should learn to distinguish the English and Australian accents. It really isn't that hard.

4. Hollywood will be required occasionally to cast English actors as the good guys.

5. You should relearn your original national anthem, "God Save The Queen", but only after fully carrying out task 1. We would not want you to get confused and give up half way through.

6. You should stop playing American "football". There is only one kind of football (proper football). What you refer to as American "football" is not a very good game. The 2.15% of you who are aware that there is a world outside your borders may have noticed that no one else plays "American" football. You will no longer be allowed to play it, and should instead play proper football. Initially, it would be best if you played with the girls. It is a difficult game. Those of you brave enough will, in time, be allowed to play rugby (which is similar to American "football", but does not involve stopping for a rest every twenty seconds or wearing full kevlar body armour like nancies). We are hoping to get together at least a US rugby sevens side by 2025.

7. You should declare war on Quebec and France, using nuclear weapons if they give you any merde. The 98.85% of you who were not aware that there is a world outside your borders should count yourselves lucky. The Russians have never been the bad guys. "Merde" is French for "shit".

8. July 4th is no longer a public holiday. November 8th will be a new national holiday, but only in England. It will be called "Indecisive Day".

9. All American cars are hereby banned. They are crap and it is for your own good. When we show you German (proper) cars, you will understand what we mean.

10. Please tell us who killed JFK. It's been driving us crazy.

------- oooOooo ------

26 - The Startrek Page

It's refereeing Jim, but not as we know it

Just how do referees cope with some of the strange things that happen in the game today?

It happened in the Aylesbury District League a couple of seasons ago. Both teams are lined up ready for the kick-off when the referee's count-up reveals that the home side has twelve players on the pitch. He calls the home captain across. The skipper admits that he isn't sure who shouldn't be on, "It's the managers decision and he's still in the dressing room." At that he sprints off to the pavilion.

As soon as he's out of view, the ref, now happy that he has two eleven-sided teams, blows up for the start of the game. The visitor's kick-off and as they make their first forages the home skipper re-appears with manager in tow. He's not happy that the game has started without him, and even less happy when the referee says that as he's not one of the named substitutes he'll not be playing any part in this game. Suffice to say that the referee had a difficult time keeping control thereafter.

Then there are those moments that every referee has at some time when they wish they were anywhere but on that particular pitch at that time so 'Beam Me Up Scottie'.

Eduardo Angel Pazos was a courageous football referee, he refused to be intimidated by the partisan home crowd when refereeing the Peru v Argentina match in 1964. With just two minutes to go the Peruvians equalised and their supporters went crazy with delight. Until, that is, Pazos disallowed the goal and then they just went crazy.

His decision sparked off a mass riot which ended with 301 dead, over 500 injured and every window in the Lima stadium broken. Afterwards with tear gas still wafting over the ground, Pazos was pressed for a comment on his decision. 'Maybe it was a goal," he said, 'anyone can make a mistake.'

27 - Referee Quiz Time

So you think you could be a really good referee do you? You think that it can't be that difficult do you? Well first you have to know the Laws of the Game. If you get any wrong you cannot referee a match.

1. What is the minimum height of a corner flag?

2. A defender tries to clear the ball behind for a corner kick but the ball rebounds from the corner flag back into play. What is the decision of the referee?

3. A substitute enters the field during stoppage in play. Where does he enter the field of play?

4. What is the minimum number of players required by a team to start a match?

5. A player cannot be offside from three types of set piece. Name all three.

6. As soon as the referee blows his whistle for a penalty kick to be taken, can the goalkeeper move off his goal line?

7. Must a penalty be a shot at goal?

8. The ball enters an opponents goal directly after having been thrown by an attacking player. What is your decision?

9. What choice does the team winning the toss-up have?

10. At a goal kick when is the ball considered to be in play?

11. What is the difference between a direct and an indirect free kick and how does the referee signal the difference?

12. Is obstruction a direct or an indirect free kick offence?

13. Name the 9 things that the referee must take on to the pitch with him at the start of every match?

Answers are at the back of the book

------- oooOooo ------

28 - Old News

A look back at some news cuttings about refereeing and the Laws of the Game

Monday, 22 November 2010

Fixtures in Scotland face possible postponement next weekend after Category One referees facing the biggest threat to their safety since Duncan Ferguson retired, voted to strike after being refused permission by the Scottish Premier League to wear balaclavas.

Scottish match officials are upset at the dangerously high level of criticism that has come their way this season and hoped the disguise could prevent the possibility of angry supporters with an eye for conceit recognizing them in the street.

The Scottish Football Association (SFA) released a statement saying the proposals were ridiculous and could place some of the most vulnerable people in Scottish society in extreme danger.

'The drug and alcohol problems in Scotland are well documented, as are the high crime levels. Balaclavas and crime go hand in hand. They are the stealing classes trademark and the last thing we want is for football fans to mistake criminals in the course of their duty for referees and exact violent revenge upon their being.'

'That should be left to the police. Or Duncan Ferguson. Or whoever gets there first.'

Scottish referee Willie Boyd expressed surprise at the statement.

'The flippant refusal to address the fears of top level Scottish referees is indicative of the malaise within the SFA. They have been listening to our pleas for years yet we have seen no action.'

'In fact, I'd say Steven Hawking's exercise bike had seen more action.'

The SFA have said they are considering hiring the services of referees from the South Korean League, who are martial arts experts.

Friday, 25 February 2011

Soccer's President Sepp Blatter has announced that starting from next year referees will be issued with additional cards to the current yellows and reds.

Two additional cards, a green and a white, will be needed because of the new 'sin-bin' rule coming in designed to significantly reduce the shirt pulling, and pushing in the box during corners type of offences. From next year referees will be able to show a green card to players - meaning they have to leave the field of play for any amount of time the referee deems appropriate - with a white card then later shown to inform the player he can return to the pitch.

"Players will not be told how long they are to sit on the benches" explained Mr Blatter "They will not know until they see that white card. In fact the referee might decide not to show the white card later at all.

"Any number of players could be sin-binned to the benches during a match so clearly there is going to be a great reduction in the offences we're trying to stamp out. Let's be under no illusions, when a professional player pulls an opponents shirt or pushes them about in the box during a corner what they are basically doing is cheating - admitting they don't consider themselves talented enough to score a goal or to stop a goal from being scored through their abilities alone.

And what does that lead to? It reduces the overall amount of goals being scored in any match which in turn reduces the entertainment to the paying spectator - the people who pay a lot of money to watch ninety minutes of top class football. "

Most will agree. Nobody enjoys seeing a goal scored against the team one's supporting but the frustration of watching a goal scoring opportunity come to nothing because of a tug on a shirt by a cheat is also not enjoyable. Most spectators prefer to see a game finish 1-1 than 0-0.

"The rule will also give referees the option of showing a green card instead of a second yellow with the current automatic red" explained Mr Blatter.

"At the moment there are occasions whereby a player shown a second yellow still hasn't really deserved to be sent off, and sometimes referees may not show a second yellow simply because they know it means having to follow it with a red." "We did also discuss the possibility of widening the goal posts as a way of increasing overall the numbers of goals being scored but we feel this sin-bin method alone should suffice."

------- oooOooo ------

29 - Extra Time

Short extracts that didn't fit well anywhere else or as the film industry would term them - 'Cuttings'.

DISSENT

Heard the one about the referee who started a match with only ten men in one team who indicated that their eleventh member would be arriving very shortly by helicopter. After five minutes play a chopper circles overhead before landing in the centre circle. The eleventh member climbs out already kitted out and takes his place on the wing. The referee approaches and promptly cautions the player and shows the yellow card. "What's that for ref?" asks the newcomer. "Descent" is the reply.

THE 4th OFFICIAL

The main role of the fourth official is to assist the teams in yelling "REF" when they want a substitution.

ASSESSSMENT

After having a real stinker of a game, the referee said cheerfully to the assessor: "I suppose you've seen worse referees in your time?" There wasn't a flicker of a reply. "I suppose that you've seen worse referees in your tie?" shouted the referee. "I heard you the first time," said the assessor, "I'm just trying to remember when!"

IN OLDEN DAYS DISSENT STILL EXISTED

John Lewis was considered to be the best referee during the early period of football. He refereed the FA Cup Finals of 1895, 1897 and 1898. He later wrote that he was the victim of a great deal of hostility: "For myself, I would take no objection to hooting or groaning by the spectators at decisions with which they disagree. The referee should remember that football is a game that warms the blood of player and looker-on alike, and that unless they can give free vent to their delight or anger, as the case may be, the great crowds we now witness will dwindle rapidly away."

HEAVY RAIN

A match between two non-League teams took place last winter in the North of England. It had been raining heavily all week and the ground resembled a swamp.

However, the referee ruled that play was possible and tossed the coin to determine ends.

The visiting captain won the toss and, after a moment's thought, said, 'OK - we'll take the shallow end!'

OFFSIDE DEFINITIONS

Definition 1: The offside rule is there to attract to football those people who can already explain how to play cricket

Definition 2: A player is offside if they are nearer to the opponent's goal line than both the ball and the second last player - except on alternate Saturdays when in addition the second last player must be facing in the opposite goals direction in which the ball is directed.

Definition 3: A player is not offside if they are in their own half of the field, or they are level with the second last opponent, or the player, opponent and referee form a triangle as perceived by an imaginary linesmen positioned on the Celestial Meridian.

Definition 4: All offside regulations are immediately found to be in favour of the defending team if shortly after the ball is played they all stop, in unison, and raise their right arm to the linesman and appeal for an offside decision.

THE 5-9 BATTLE

I was always taught as a referee to get a tight and early hold on the confrontations at both ends of the pitch between the centre-forward and the opposing centre-half, the numbers 5 and 9. I recall once when nothing appeared to be going on between two well known protagonists occupying these shirts that I pulled them together and said that I had seen what they were up to and they were on thin ice. They both apologised and trudged meekly away.

REALLY HAPPENED

Corner to the Red team, as the ball comes over the Red attacker screams "BOO". I blew up for off-putting of an opponent and asked the player to explain his outburst. He said that he was trying to scare the birds out of the nearby tree, When do they think we were born?

APOLOGY

Sorry but the referee at our match didn't do anything silly, controversial or daft to warrant a story here. That was because he called the game off as soon as he turned up as the pitch was unplayable in his opinion. Well there were a couple of families of gypo's parked on it so I guess he had a point. That never happens at Old Trafford!

------- oooOooo ------

30 - Problem Page

Agony Uncle, Jeff the Ref, lends a sympathetic and advisory ear to problems from referees

Dear Jeff

I have been reffing for a few months now but have still to caution my first player. There have been occasions when I know that a player has deserved a yellow card but I can't seem to bring myself to perform the actual act. I think it's because there is an audience and I'm naturally shy and retiring.

Rodney, Bradford

Answer: This is quite a common complaint Rodney, sometimes referred to as Yellow Fever. However there is a known cure. Once you get over the initial caution you will be fine. Can I suggest that upon arrival at a ground you claim to hear one of the changing away team players complaining about the referee. As the player leaves the changing room, it doesn't matter which one, anyone will do, take him to one side and issue the caution for dissent with no witnesses around. You've got your first victim and I guarantee before that game is over you will have booked or sent off several more visiting players.

Dear Jeff

I was appointed to a F.A. Vase tie in Oldham last January when the away team's colours were very dark blue shirts and black shorts. What should I have worn?

Colour Conscious, Manchester

Answer: *Wellies*

Dear Jeff

I've only been reffing a couple of months but it hasn't been going so well as I've got this feeling that everybody hates me at every game I've been to so far. Can you help me?

Grade 3, Leeds

Answer: *You say that everybody hates you and that's not easy to achieve as normally the winning team think that you are great. Doesn't seem like you've got a problem to me as you appear to be making excellent strides. I shall watch your progress with interest as you are obviously destined for greater things.*

Dear Jeff

Black is not really my colour but the County F.A. wont allow me to wear an alternative. It's getting to the stage where I am seriously considering handing back my whistle.

Deidre, Oxford

Answer: Have you thought about more colourful accessories - red tee shirt, green whistle, multi-coloured notebook, yellow scarf, carnation button-hole? Let your mind wander, don't be inhibited by tradition.

Dear Jeff

My 29 years old brother is the Referees' Appointments Secretary for the League that I referee in. He repeatedly allocates me games between teams top and bottom of the divisions, those that are going to end up 10-0, the boring one-sided games. Then I also get those teams that have a reputation for intimidating and abusing match officials, where they have a history of assaulting referees. I never get the prime competitive games we all crave for. I am 32 years old. Do you think I should tell our mum?

Answer: I most certainly do. Being the younger brother he will have, no doubt, 'told on you' many times in the past and it's time you got your own back on him. It's no good turning to official channels as they will not be as effective as the maternal route. Go to it my son.

------- oooOooo ------

I hope that you've enjoyed at least some of the content of my first book. If you have, please tell your friends and post a review on Amazon. If you haven't enjoyed any of it, keep schtum, don't cross the ref!

Jeff Jacklin

Quiz Answers

1. What is the minimum height of a corner flag? ANSWER: 5 feet

2. A defender tries to clear the ball behind for a corner kick but the ball rebounds from the corner flag back into play. What is the decision of the referee? ANSWER: Play-on, the ball is still in play.

3. A substitute enters the field during stoppage in play. Where does he enter the field of play? ANSWER: From the touchline at the half-way line.

4. What is the minimum number of players required by a team to start a match? ANSWER: 7

5. A player cannot be offside from three types of set piece. Name all three. ANSWER: Goal-kick, throw-in and corner-kick.

6. As soon as the referee blows his whistle for a penalty kick to be taken, can the goalkeeper move off his goal line? ANSWER: No he must wait until the ball has been kicked by the penalty taker.

7. Must a penalty be a shot at goal? ANSWER: No but it has to be kicked forward.

8. The ball enters an opponent's goal directly after having been thrown by an attacking player. What is your decision? ANSWER: Goal kick.

9. What choice does the team winning the toss-up have? ANSWER: They have choice of which end to defend. The team losing the toss has to take the kick-off.

10. At a goal kick when is the ball considered to be in play? ANSWER: Once it has left the penalty area.

11. What is the difference between a direct and an indirect free kick and how does the referee signal the difference? ANSWER: A goal can be

scored directly from a direct free-kick whereas it cannot from an indirect one. The referee signals an indirect free-kick by raising his arm straight up.

12. Is obstruction a direct or an indirect free kick offence? ANSWER: Indirect

13. Name the 9 things that the referee must take on to the pitch with him at the start of every match? ANSWER: Whistle, notepad, pen (or pencil), yellow card, red card, coin, watch, spare watch, football.